BUSINESS ETIQUETTE

BUSINESS ETIQUETTE

Make a good impression — gain the competitive edge

Jacqueline Dunckel

Self-Counsel Press
(*a division of*)
International Self-Counsel Press Ltd.
Canada   U.S.A.

Printed in Canada

First edition: November, 1987
Second edition: August, 1992

Cataloguing in Publication Data
Dunckel, Jacqueline, 1930-
    Business etiquette

    (Self-counsel business series)
    First ed. published as: Business etiquette today.
    ISBN 0-88908-531-5

    1. Business etiquette. 2. Table etiquette. I. Title. II. Title:
Business etiquette today. III. Series.
HF5389.D86 1992 395'.52 C92-091564-7

Cover photograph by Terry Guscott

Self-Counsel Press
(a division of)
International Self-Counsel Press Ltd.

1481 Charlotte Road   1704 N. State Street
North Vancouver, British Columbia   Bellingham, Washington
V7J 1H1   98225

CONTENTS

FIGURES

With special thanks to my mother, Bernice Nowlin, and my daughter, Nancy Dunckel, who contributed from either side of my generation.

INTRODUCTION

This handbook is written for quick, easy access to basic information on practical business etiquette. More detailed books on social etiquette are readily available — but they won't fit easily into your briefcase!

The book is based on two premises:

(a) In business, everyone — subordinate, peer, or superior should be treated with equal courtesy and respect.

(b) Business etiquette rules are the same for men and women.

So how do these premises affect the content of this book?

Good manners begin with self-respect. When you respect yourself you have thoughtful concern for yourself and act with appropriate behavior. When you respect yourself, you naturally treat others with the same consideration you would expect from them in return.

When you act with considerate respect, you will react appropriately: no woman will lose her femininity, and no man will be less masculine. People help each other when help is needed. If a man is going down a hall, his arms loaded, a woman behind him should move ahead, open and hold the door for him. He should do the same for her in a similar situation. Gender and business position are not considerations. A person who has self-respect can accept and perform common courtesies.

But this also means that some traditions need to be abandoned when male executives deal with the new female executives. "Acts of chivalry" such as always picking up the bill in a restaurant; of feeling compelled to rush ahead to hold the door for her; of standing up when a woman arrives late in the meeting, and then helping seat her; of getting off the elevator last to allow the woman behind to leave the car first are no longer "correct" behavior.

In today's business world, whoever is closest to the door gets off the elevator first. A woman puts on her own coat, and a man puts on his own coat, but if either of them is having trouble, one should quickly move to help the other.

No one should withhold common courtesy from anyone else as a way of making a political statement. Women should not only open their own doors, but hold doors open for others, whether male or female. Men should go on being gracious. The graciousness is not based on the sex of the recipient. If you, as a man, encounter a woman who finds it difficult to accept your graciousness gracefully, you should consider her unpleasantness as a failing on her part, not on yours. Men and women must realize that courtesy and consideration are virtues that should remain outside the battleground of the sexes.

Business etiquette means give and take, helping each other when help is needed, and being considerate of others. Social etiquette, however, has its own traditional set of rules. This book deals with business etiquette. I use host for host or hostess and chair for chairman/chairperson as generic terms.

Before you begin reading through this book, keep these three basic rules in mind. Think of them as a "quick fix" for good business etiquette:

(a) Use the golden rule — treat others, all others, as you would wish to be treated yourself.

(b) Use the five magic words too often neglected in business: Please, Thank you, Well done.

(c) Like oil and water, drugs, booze, and business do not mix.

1

TO BEGIN AT THE BEGINNING —
THE ETIQUETTE OF EMPLOYMENT

In business, just like everywhere else, first impressions are important and lasting. Whether you are looking for a job or are in the position of hiring someone new, you should be especially conscious of your manners throughout the employment interview. You might have all the qualifications, but if you leave a poor impression, you won't be offered the job. Similarly, if you don't represent your company well, you may never find good employees to work for you.

WHEN YOU ARE BEING INTERVIEWED

Wherever you go, remember to smile; it will put you at ease and others will respond in kind. Remember, however, that a constant smile restricts your face and appears phony.

1. As you arrive
- Treat all company personnel, from the security guard to the receptionist, with consideration. A good company respects the opinion of all its staff. The impression you make starts on the telephone or as you walk into the building.

- Arrive at least 10 minutes before the appointed time.

- Arrive prepared. When you leave material "at home" it gives the impression you did not care enough to prepare for the interview. Do your homework about the company.

- Your appearance and good grooming should reflect respect for yourself, your occupation, and the position you desire. People who care about their appearance give the impression they care about their jobs and about the company they work for. Well-groomed hair, well-shined shoes, appropriate dress, minimum accessories, and subtle shaving lotion or scent all add up to a good company image.

- Pay close attention to personal hygiene: mouthwash, deodorant, and manicured hands are essential.

2. **During the interview**

- Your first words to an interviewer should be "thank you" in consideration of the time spent on you.

- Always remember to shake hands.

- Do not take a seat until invited to do so.

- Sit up straight. Keep your hands apart (no fiddling).

- Look the interviewer in the eye.

- Do not pick up anything on the interviewer's desk.

- Do not try to read anything on the desk.

- Do not call a woman interviewer "ma'am," "my dear," or anything that suggests gender unless she has been referred to or refers to herself as Miss, Mrs., or Ms.

- Speak to be heard. Reply with thought, honesty, and enthusiasm. Positive listener response to a vocal message is mainly due to facial expression and vocal tone.

- Listen! Focus. Respond succinctly.

- Do not speak ill of others or another company.

- Have a good pen and pad readily available to take notes.

- Watch your gestures. Body language can be offensive and indicate poor manners. Never point your finger in an accusing manner; a sprawling posture shows disrespect for the people with you.

3. Leaving the interview

- Watch for signals that the interview is over.

- Before leaving, reinforce, in one sentence, your desire to work for the firm. Do not plead, beg, or whine: just make a positive statement.

- Shake hands. Smile.

- Exit gracefully, with positive posture.

4. After the interview

Immediately after the interview, write a letter of thanks to the interviewer expressing your interest in the job and your appreciation for the time given you. Tell in your own words how much it would mean to be employed by the company. Be sure to write a thank-you letter to anyone who allowed you to make a call or wrote a letter on your behalf.

Do not pester an employer for a job. It is all right to call back within a month if you have not heard, and you may call back in several months to let them know you are still interested if any positions come open.

WHEN YOU ARE INTERVIEWING

1. Before the interview

If you receive unsolicited resumes, you don't have to interview them but it is bad manners not to respond. If you advertise a position, it is not necessary to contact any people who respond except those you wish to interview. While this is accepted business practice, it is considered exceptionally good etiquette to at least acknowledge all responses to an advertisement.

It is only good manners to let your department or the people who will be working with a new employee know that you are interviewing. It is bad manners to keep the interviewee waiting. Come out of your office to greet the person or have the secretary or receptionist bring the interviewee to your office.

Shake hands with the person and extend full business and professional courtesy (e.g., hang up coat, indicate chair). Set the same tone the person would find while working in the office — conservative or less traditional — whatever reflects reality. Ensure that there will be no interruptions so you can give your full attention to the interview.

2. During the interview

- Sit in a businesslike manner. Don't slump or lean back in the chair; sit in an active listening posture.

- Make good eye contact.

- Do not fiddle with things on your desk.

4

- Do not call the interviewee "ma'am," "Miss," "boy," or anything that suggests gender, unless using Miss, Mrs., Ms., Mr., followed by his or her surname. After the initial greeting, use first names.

- Let the person know what to call you.

- Wear the same clothes that are acceptable any other time in the office.

- Be well groomed. You represent the company. To attract good personnel, you must reflect the company in the best possible light. Clean, well-groomed hair, clothing, shoes and nails along with use of mouthwash and deodorant is essential.

- Speak to be heard. Keep questions short and to the point. Clarify if necessary.

- Listen! Focus on what the person is saying rather than on your next question.

- Bring the interview to a satisfactory close so that the interviewee knows it is over.

- Indicate when he or she will hear from you.

- Shake hands. See the person out.

3. After the interview

Let the interviewee know within two weeks after the interview what is happening. When the position has been filled, write a letter to the job applicant. Do not discuss job applicants outside the parameters of your office and your job function.

5

| **WHEN YOU'VE** | • | Ask questions but don't pry into personal lives. |
| **BEEN HIRED** | | |

- Don't discuss your fears or concerns.
- Don't tell everyone how "we did it at my old job."
- Don't ally yourself with any one person or group. Be friendly, but take your time to get to know people. Be amiable toward everyone in the company.
- Don't listen to gossip.
- Be sure to thank those who have been helpful.

WHEN YOU HIRE SOMEONE

- Introduce new employees to other employees as soon as possible and make them feel at home.
- Link them to someone else who can carry on the introductions.

(For more information on hiring procedures, see *A Small Business Guide to Employee Selection*, another title in the Self-Counsel Series.)

FIRING AND BEING FIRED

So much of the firing process involves human rights, union agreements, and legal precedence. You may want legal advice before you fire anyone, or you may want legal help if you are being fired. But in either case, although firing is usually unpleasant and emotionally upsetting, good etiquette can help ease the way.

1. Firing

- If you have to fire someone, your manner should be businesslike. You should never get into personal issues.
- Keep the meeting short and completely private. Don't stall or chat. Be kind, firm, and constructive.

	• Keep what is said confidential.
2. Being fired	• Conduct yourself with dignity. Maintain your self-respect.
	• Get on with your career. Don't gripe or cry to fellow workers.
	• If you feel the firing is unjust, let your lawyer or union speak for you.

2

DEPARTMENT DECORUM

Your good manners let bosses, peers, and staff know that you are self-confident, professional, caring, and dedicated. Let's look at some basic considerations before we deal with specifics.

THE BASICS

- Swearing is unacceptable in business. So is crying, shouting, or other manifestations of loss of temper.

- Don't visit and chat when you're not busy. "Standing around the water cooler" can mark you as a lazy employee. As well, don't read magazines or indulge in personal business when you're not busy. Get busy!

- Don't entertain friends in your office.

- Don't drop into someone else's office unannounced. Call first. If someone drops into your office to chat, stand up and move toward the door letting them know you are busy. Be friendly, polite, but firm.

- Leave your bad mood at the door. Don't take it out on others. Don't put others down.

- Don't borrow money, equipment, or supplies from the workplace unless absolutely necessary. If you do borrow something, return it promptly.

8

- Don't be heard around the office complaining about problems, other people, or your lack of promotion. Arrange to meet with the people who should hear what you have to say.

- Don't use nicknames in business.

- Keep personal office decor to a minimum and in good taste.

- Keep your personal life and your business life separate.

- Keep confidences, both professional and personal.

- Above all, don't gossip

CLEARING THE AGENDA

Let's get the business of fingers, pens, pencils, plastic stirrers, toothpicks, foam cups, and sound effects out of the way.

It would seem unthinkable that anyone would conduct personal hygiene practices in public, but the number of executives who pick noses, probe ears and teeth with pens and pencils, clip or file nails, suck teeth, scratch scalps, chew cuticles, probe, and rearrange is appalling.

Others consider knuckle cracking, flatulence, belching, uncovered yawns, and sneezes publicly appropriate. Not so boorish, but equally annoying, is public use of the toothpick which is then left in the mouth; chewing toothpicks, pens and pencils, ties, scarves and gum; plastic stirrers, accordion pleated and chewed; and plastic foam cups that are chewed, drawn upon or sculpted with pens and fingernails.

In a word, DON'T.

If someone does any of the above in your presence, you have every right to ask him or her to stop. Do so in private. Point out that noses, ears, and other body parts should be attended to in private. Regard for others includes body emissions and sounds.

- Teeth should be attended to in the washroom and the pick immediately discarded.

- If you have a Picasso of plastic in your office, invest in china cups and real spoons for use at meetings.

- Don't chew gum. (Early in my life I stopped chewing gum when I was told "The gum chewing girl and the cud chewing cow are something alike yet different somehow. It must be the intelligent look on the face of the cow.")

- Keep your hands away from your face and hair.

- Don't eat food at your desk except for exceptional situations.

- Abide by the smoking rules of the company.

- Don't put on make-up or repair manicures at your desk.

- Don't discuss body parts or body functions.

- Don't sit on anyone else's desk.

- Keep your feet on the floor. They should not be put on desks, tables, or chairs.

OFFICE UPS AND DOWNS, INS AND OUTS

When to sit and when to stand may seem a small issue, but it is a basic business manners conundrum, along with meeting and greeting, and opening doors.

1. **Ups and downs**
   - Visitors from outside the business should be escorted to and from their appointments unless they call quite frequently. Visitors are escorted by

either the secretary or the person they are meeting. The visitor follows the escort.

- It is a mark of respect for a secretary to rise to greet a visitor from outside the firm.

- Rise from your chair and come around your desk to shake hands with your visitor.

- Rise from your chair when a superior enters your office. It shows professional respect.

- In a meeting or boardroom, it is not necessary to keep standing up and sitting down.

2. **Ins and outs**
- The person closest to the door of a crowded elevator gets off first and the rest follow. Follow the same routine for getting on the elevator. If the elevator is very crowded, it is good manners to press the open button until everyone is in.

- If you are near the button panel, ask what floors are wanted and punch accordingly.

- First to the door is first through. But, if the door pulls toward you, you may wish to hold the door for those behind you. Junior executives certainly should do so for senior executives and for visitors.

- Go through the revolving door first if you are first to get to it. When you have guests with you, wait for them on the other side.

CO-WORKERS

How you treat your co-workers will make a big difference in how well you get on in your job. Remember that everyone is important from the mail clerk to the chief executive officer (CEO), and should be treated with consideration and respect. Whether they work for you or you work for them shouldn't make a difference in how you treat them.

- Compliment people on a job well done. Compliments must be genuine and sincere.

- Don't ever comment on someone's physical beauty or handsomeness.

- No one should be called "boy" or "girl" after the age of puberty. "Honey" and "hunk" are not acceptable either. (See chapter 13 for more discussion of issues of sexual harassment.)

- Senior executives should not be called "sir" or "ma'am." Use Mr., Mrs., Miss, or Ms. until asked to do otherwise.

- Always let people know what you would like to be called. Keep your position and the relationship in mind.

- Greet co-workers and return greetings. Once a day is enough. If you keep running into them in the hall, nod and smile.

- Never reprimand anyone in front of others: do so in private.

- Respect another's privacy. Don't listen in on another's phone calls or conversations. Don't read papers on anyone else's desk.

- Don't "look" for anything on anyone else's desk. Ask a secretary to find the material or wait until the person returns.

- It is bad manners to ask co-workers to cover for you.

- It is not bad manners to ask politely for less noise or privacy or to let people know you have work to do and haven't time to chat.

- If two people are arguing, stay out of it.

- If you ever lose your temper, apologize immediately.

1. Receptionists

Receptionists are the first image of a company. They are the front-line public relations people. A company's good manners are judged by the actions of the receptionist. The reception area should be clean and well maintained. It should not be a gathering place for chit chat. The receptionist must discourage it.

A receptionist of a multinational company or a receptionist who deals with many foreign clients should be able to converse in the native tongue of the country in which the office is located as well as the language of any foreign offices and of the most predominant clients. In a bilingual country, the receptionist of a national company should speak both languages, unaccented.

If you are a receptionist —

- Be cordial, well-spoken, and polite. Greet people with a smile and act professionally.

- While on the job, do not eat, chew gum, chat or gossip with co-workers.

- Do not make remarks like "turkey" or "jerk," after hanging up the phone.

- Keep well informed on the company's business and the function of its personnel.

- Say the name of the company clearly and concisely, no matter how often you say it.

- Call everyone by their last name and maintain an air of dignity and decorum.

- If a visitor is kept waiting, be solicitous.

If you work with a receptionist —

- Treat her with respect.

- Realize the receptionist is vitally important to your company's image and its smooth operation.

2. Secretaries

Establish the ground rules with your secretary at the start. Discuss how you will address each other. Review job duties and what they include; avoid the "who makes the coffee" hassle.

Remember that secretaries and bosses are social equals outside the business office. It is poor manners to fall into your professional roles if you happen to meet socially, but the social aspect should not affect office decorum.

If you are a secretary —

- Confidentiality is essential.

- If a boss is a poor communicator, it is only good business etiquette to ask specific questions that will allow you to complete a task successfully.

- It is good manners for you to remind your boss about writing a business thank you.

- Even if you call each other by your first names, it is more businesslike to be formal when you have visitors.

If a secretary works for you —

- Don't become friends with your secretary. However, while private lives should remain private, there are times when you may wish to inform one another of changes in your life (e.g., divorce or illness). Keep it short and businesslike.

- Never ask a secretary to lie for you.

- Treat all secretaries as the professionals they are.

- Give praise and credit when due.

- It is bad manners to ask a secretary to complete personal errands.

- It is good manners to let your secretary know where you are at all times during business hours.

3. **Bosses and staff**
   - The higher the position the better the manners should be. Set the example.

   - If insulted by a superior in front of others, do not retaliate. If you feel strongly enough, and it will not jeopardize your career, request a private meeting.

- As a boss, you show extreme self-confidence by apologizing if you inadvertently insult someone.

- If you are leaving a position, discuss it privately with your immediate boss before submitting your resignation.

- If you feel you have been bypassed for a position, do not complain to your peers. Instead, discuss the matter with your superior, privately.

- If you are in the boss's office when another executive comes in, it is up to the boss to ask you to remain or leave.

- It is up to the superior to let people know what he or she wishes to be called.

- Treat employees as employees, not children.

FRIENDS AND LOVERS

- Keep friendships separate from work.

- Do not become indebted to a co-worker or employee.

- It is not only poor etiquette, but dangerous to pursue sexual affairs in business. They can jeopardize careers, disrupt work, and cause scandal. If it will hurt no one and will not interfere with your job — okay. But don't talk about it. There are times when one of you may have to move within the company or to another job. Be ready for these possibilities.

- Don't get involved in anyone else's office romance.

- Don't take sides in a romantic argument or breakup.
- Never discuss your sex life at the office.

CLIENTS AND CUSTOMERS

If you are a client or customer visiting another business, you expect consideration from a well-mannered staff. But remember your own manners too.

- Be punctual.
- Never be defensive.
- Be loyal.
- Always call in advance.
- Smile and shake hands on arrival and departure.
- Present your card to the receptionist, but don't hound him or her. Sit quietly and wait for your appointment.

If you are on the other side, often greeting and meeting clients, manners are extra important. People want to do business with a company that shows respect and consideration. Good manners can mean bigger profits.

- Be discreet. Never gossip about one client to another.
- With a new client, shake hands. Place your card on the desk. The client will usually reciprocate.
- Be sure to hang up visitors' coats.
- You may offer tea or coffee.
- Always accompany your client out to the reception area or elevator.
- If you have to keep someone waiting, advise and apologize yourself, have your secretary do so, or let the receptionist know.

OFFICE DIPLOMACY

Business diplomacy differs from etiquette or manners. It can either save or advance your career.

There are four words to avoid to be a true business diplomat: "yes," "no," "never," and "always."

- "Yes" and "no" allow for no change or maneuvering. (You'll note that politicians very rarely use these words.) Give yourself time to consider before you commit yourself or your department.

- "Never" and "always" can box you into a position you have to prove "We never make mistakes," or label your professional style "We always do it this way."

If you ever have to criticize, don't be personal, always give a reason for the criticism backed by proof, and ask questions to get more information. Base your criticism on the good of the project and the company. Suggest change or try to help solve the situation but don't take on the job yourself.

If your own work is criticized, don't take it personally, don't blame anyone else or make excuses, and ask questions in a non-defensive manner. Be open to suggestions and thank the person who gave helpful criticism.

Don't ever discuss criticism with the rest of the office.

3

MANNERS FOR THE TELEPHONE AND OTHER ELECTRONIC DEVICES

Over 50% of all business is done over the telephone. How you present yourself on the phone is a reflection of your company. Keep in mind that when you talk on the telephone, you have to convey both your personality and your attitude to the listener, since the listener cannot see your expression. If you have a flat, monotonous voice, for example, you'll want to work at making it sound more lively, especially for talking to people you have never met before.

TELEPHONE BASICS

- Be professional. "Honey" and "my dear" have no place in business.

- Never say "yeah" or "okay." Use "yes" and "certainly."

- Don't tuck the phone under your chin. Speak directly and articulate clearly.

- You don't have to speak louder for long distance calls unless you have a poor connection. In that case, hang up and try again.

- Sound enthusiastic. If you have to answer the phone a lot, keep a mirror near the phone. Smile before you answer so there will be a smile in your voice.

- Listen attentively.

- Answer as promptly as possible.

- Do not put people on hold unless absolutely necessary. If the wait is going to be longer than a minute, let the caller know and suggest they call back.

- Be courteous to wrong numbers, to the rude, or to the misinformed.

- Let an angry person defuse before trying to discuss the situation. Don't lose your own temper.

- You have every right to hang up on someone who uses profanity. It is against the law to swear on the telephone.

- Secretaries and receptionists should not "sing" the company name.

- Calls should be returned the day they are received or as soon as possible.

- If you are cut off, it is correct for the caller to call back.

- The one who places the call terminates the call. The exception is when the caller forgets this point of etiquette and talks on and on.

- If you have difficulty understanding a person's name, ask for the spelling.

- If you are in a co-worker's office when a call comes in for the other person, signal you are going for coffee and quietly excuse yourself. If the co-worker indicates you should stay, focus your attention away from the person and the call.

- Please, don't have music or a radio station playing on the line when you put someone on hold. This technique is in poor taste and is bad manners.

WHEN YOU CALL

- Identify yourself immediately and leave your name and number if the person is not available. Spell your name.

- Do not ask where the person is when he or she is not available.

- Don't make personal phone calls. If they are necessary, keep them short.

- Do not call back on the same day if you have left your name and number. Call again only in an emergency.

- When leaving a call on an answering machine, give the date, time you called, name, company number, and a short message.

- Do not show annoyance when you are asked to wait.

- When making personal calls to a business friend, consider the time of day. Keep the call short.

- Be very polite when calling a friend's place of business. The friend's reputation is at stake.

- Always ask if it is a convenient time to call.

- Do not eat, drink, smoke, or shuffle papers when on the phone.

- Sit up straight. Speak directly into the mouthpiece.

- Only call employees at home when it is absolutely necessary.

- Do not be put out if asked to state your business. Explain succinctly.

- If you haven't been able to reach someone, ask when it would be a good time to call.

- If you dial a wrong number, apologize and hang up.

- If you are put on hold and they fail to return after two minutes, hang up and call back. Keep calm. It is very poor manners to lose your temper.

- When your secretary makes the call for you, if the person is in, you should be on the line when he or she picks up the phone.

WHEN THE CALL IS FOR YOU

Many executives ask their secretaries or receptionists to ask who is calling. The premise for this practice is that it utilizes the executive's time more efficiently. However, to the caller, it can give the impression that calls are being screened.

If it is being used for the former reason, then the secretary or receptionist may ask, "May I have your name so I can tell Mr. or Ms. So and So who is calling?"

If being used for the latter, to screen, then it is very poor business etiquette and the practice should be discontinued. You are either available or you are not. Don't have your secretary play games for you. If you don't want to take calls, you are "in a meeting" until you can return the calls.

Here are some other points to keep in mind when you are receiving calls.

- Answer promptly and with your full name.

- If the call does not go through a switchboard or your secretary,

22

answer with the company name, the department, and your full name.

- If someone calls your home, you can have the person who answers the call ask the caller to contact you at the office.

- If you are one of the numbers to be called during a business crisis, be sure your family is advised so you get the call.

WHEN THE CALL IS FOR SOMEONE ELSE

If a caller has reached the wrong person, assist him or her in getting the right party. Don't shout for the person and don't bang the phone down. If you can't find the person, don't leave the caller waiting, but take and deliver a message.

TELEPHONE CALLS, VISITORS, AND MEETINGS

- If a call comes in when office co-workers are in your office, you can let them know politely you'd like to take the call in private. Suggest they can return to their offices, get a cup of coffee, or wait outside. You can get back to them when you're finished the call.

- It is best to have all calls held when you have a guest or are in a meeting.

- If an important call comes in when people are in your office, it is best to take it in another office.

CALLS AND CLIENTS

- Use small talk to help open a conversation, but keep it to a minimum. Don't close with small talk. People remember longest what they hear last.

- Remember you want "yes" to your request, or at least "no." Don't settle for "maybe."

- Make the call with a positive attitude. Maintain that attitude and good manners even when the answer is "no."

FAXES AND ELECTRONIC MAIL

There is one basic thing to remember when using electronic communication systems: While it isn't very often a business associate might listen in on your business call, it might be easy to access voice mail. Fax messages can be picked up by someone else and computer screens are easily read over another's shoulder. Keep these points in mind.

- Whatever you put into an easily accessible message should be written or voiced in business language and tone, keeping in mind that it could be read or heard by someone other than for whom it was intended.

- If you should intercept a message that is intended for someone else, your good manners will stop you from reading or listening any further.

- If you receive a message not intended for you, ignore it. Do not repeat any of the information to anyone. Destroy the message so it cannot be read by anyone else. If it happens again, notify the parties involved that their messages are being directed incorrectly.

- When you send a confidential fax, notify the receiver that the message is coming through so that he or she, or a designate, can be there to pick it up.

4

MEETING MANNERS AND BOARD-ROOM BEHAVIOR

In recent years, business has had an overdose of meetings. Some are being held simply because "We always meet on Monday" or because an individual cannot make a decision on his or her own. Keeping this in mind, the etiquette for business meetings extends beyond how to behave in one, but whether or not to hold one at all. You should call a meeting only when you have a clear purpose. Time is indeed money. Consider the amount of time being spent by the number of meeting participants. Could the same information dealt with in a meeting be circulated by a memo instead?

If you must call a meeting, here are the do's and don'ts.

BASIC CONSIDERATIONS WHEN CALLING A MEETING

Good meeting manners means careful consideration for the scheduling of the meeting. If you suspect the meeting will be a long one, don't call it for late afternoon, or else be prepared to adjourn and continue another day. Try to avoid calling meetings the day before a long weekend, too. You'll find participants clock watching and unlikely to participate because they have plans to go away or go home. You'll find co-workers more congenial in a meeting when they don't feel rushed.

- Indicate how long the meeting will take.

- Inform participants of the meeting well in advance: two weeks for an in-house meeting; four weeks for outside participants.

- Call all the participants one week in advance to remind them of the time, place, and date of meeting.

- Invite those people to the meeting who are directly responsible for the business to be discussed and any experts whose input will be needed. However, keep the numbers workable.

- It is good manners to distribute the agenda well in advance. (Always have extra copies for the meeting itself for those who forget their notes.) Include any pertinent materials that need study or consideration before the meeting.

- Start meetings on time. This shows respect for those who are on time.

- Always introduce those who do not know one another.

- Indicate where people should sit and whether smoking will be allowed.

- If possible, hold all calls for all meeting participants. If it is a scheduled long meeting, have a break at a designated time during which participants may make calls. Reconvene the meeting at the specified time.

- The chair conducts the meeting. No matter what the level of seniority of the participants, the chair controls the meeting. The chair is center stage. How the meeting goes is a direct reflection on the chair's abilities. If you are the chair, manage the meeting with tact, diplomacy, and strength. Don't be afraid to cut off anyone who tries to dominate the discussion, becomes argumentative, or tries to use the meeting as a forum for subjects not on the agenda.

- At the end of the meeting, the chair should thank those who attended, give special thanks to those who made presentations, and thank any support staff who assisted in putting on the meeting.

- Distribute minutes within 48 hours after the meeting.

For more information on correct procedures for meetings, see *Chairing a Meeting With Confidence* and *The Minute Taker's Handbook,* two other titles in the Self-Counsel Series.

MEETING MANNERS FOR PARTICIPANTS

If you are invited to participate in a meeting, arrive on time and with your homework done. Read any material that has been sent in advance. Read the agenda, and bring any materials you need, questions you have noted, or comments you wish to make.

Once you arrive, remember these basic courtesies:

- Introduce yourself to others. If you are from outside the company, give that information.

- Seat yourself only if it is a department meeting and you have a customary seat. The chair will indicate where you may be seated.

- Sit in an alert upright position. Body language is easily read.

- Do not doodle, play with pens and pencils, make airplanes, straighten paper clips, etc.

- Really listen to what is being said.

- Ask questions if you don't understand.

- Make your comments relevant to the discussion and keep them concise.

- Do not use the meeting as a forum to blow your own horn.

- Do not smoke unless it is permitted. Be conscious of the discomfort of nonsmokers if smoking is permitted.

- Remember that the chair conducts the meeting. Whatever your level of seniority in relation to the chair, the chair is in charge. (This is frequently and rudely forgotten by senior people in meetings.)

- Pick up all your papers at the end of the meeting and place any debris in a wastepaper basket or put it in an orderly fashion so it can be collected.

- Thank the chair quietly as you leave.

- If you are from outside the company, shake hands upon departure.

1. Dress and decorum at meetings

- Dress to show respect for yourself, your profession, your position and your company.

- Do not request refreshment. Take it if it is offered. Be careful of spillage on tables, documents, yourself, and others.

- If you need to leave the meeting, excuse yourself quietly and return the same way.

2. Etiquette for making a presentation at a meeting

If you are asked to make a presentation at a meeting, you should know why the presentation is asked for. What is the purpose? Is there a business decision to be made or technical information to be exchanged? If you are not clear on the purpose, ask. You don't want to waste your own and others' valuable time by preparing incorrectly. Also find out how the meeting room will be set up for you so you can prepare your presentation for the best physical impact. It is rude to make a presentation and discuss material which only a select few can see.

Further, eye contact is vitally important to you as the presenter. If you need time to set up your presentation, tell the chair you'll need five minutes. Participants can take a stretch and not focus on you until you're ready.

Also find out who will be responsible for questions and discussion: the chair, or you, as the presenter. This information should be announced to the meeting. If you are responsible, it is poor manners for the chair to assume the role.

Be clear how much time there is for your presentation. If you go over time, the chair should remind you. It is very poor manners to go over the designated time and to ask the next presenters to shorten their presentations.

THE ETIQUETTE OF MEETING SEATING

When you attend a meeting, wait to be seated. There is a protocol you should always observe:

- If the seating is at a rectangular table, the chair sits at the end of the table farthest from the entrance to the room. If there are two entrances to the room, lock the one nearest the chair. The seats on either side of the chair are for senior management and honored guests. (See Figure #1.)

29

- The exception to this seating arrangement is when delegates from other countries attend. They may wish to be seated on the long length of the table facing the door. Their most senior member will be seated at the center with your company's equally senior person immediately opposite. The visiting company officers will be seated on either side of the senior visiting official. They will be facing your company counterparts across the table. Lesser executives fill in the sides. The end seats are usually unoccupied. Senior guests should be seated facing the entrance. Be sure to check with visitors before setting up the room for your meeting. (See Figure #2.)

- The most desirable seats are those near senior officials.

- The least desirable seat is opposite the chair because you will get the full attention of the chair. In our patriarchal culture, "father" sits at the head of the table while "mother" sits at the foot of the table. If you are placed there, stay alert and interested.

- Watch that you don't sit in segregated sexes or all one department together (unless you are making a joint presentation).

ETIQUETTE FOR TELECONFERENCE MEETINGS

Teleconferencing can be an efficient, less expensive way to do business and is becoming increasingly popular. But meeting on the phone is very different than meeting in person, and if certain rules aren't strictly obeyed, the result can be disastrous. All too often, participants interrupt each other and little gets accomplished. An interruption on a teleconference call is far more serious than one in person; very often it is difficult even to tell who is talking to whom. However, with patience and perseverance, teleconferencing can succeed.

- The initiator of the meeting introduces or "roll calls" the participants and begins the discussion as chair of the meeting. It is imperative that all participants respect the control of the chair. The chair should be the only person who speaks out without being specifically called upon.

- You may be assigned a turn to speak when you can either pass, give your opinion, or ask questions. Although you may be anxious to make your point, wait until it is your turn. Speak only when you have been addressed by the chair.

- If an organized system hasn't been initiated and you wish to speak, wait for a pause and identify yourself. Otherwise you are just a voice.

- It is bad manners to interrupt when someone is speaking

- Keep your discussion to the business at hand.

- The chair should summarize, close, and thank each participant at the end of the call.

(For more information on planning and formatting meetings, see *The Business Guide to Effective Speaking*, another title in the Self-Counsel Series.)

FIGURE #1
SEATING ARRANGEMENT FOR A BUSINESS MEETING

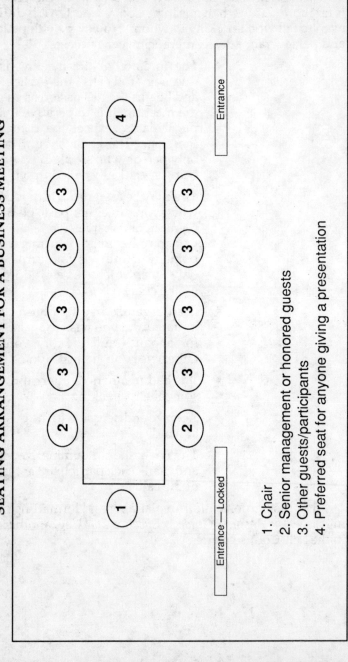

1. Chair
2. Senior management or honored guests
3. Other guests/participants
4. Preferred seat for anyone giving a presentation

32

FIGURE #2
ALTERNATE SEATING ARRANGEMENT FOR A BUSINESS MEETING

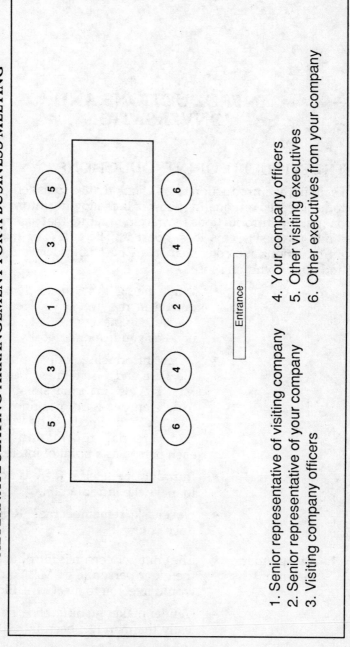

1. Senior representative of visiting company
2. Senior representative of your company
3. Visiting company officers
4. Your company officers
5. Other visiting executives
6. Other executives from your company

33

5

INTRODUCTIONS AND CONVERSATION

THE ETIQUETTE OF INTRODUCTIONS

I said in the introduction to this book that business etiquette today is based on equality. Some of the following information on making introductions may seem to refute that statement, while the rest seems to support it. The rules for making introductions and conversation are based on social etiquette and good common sense.

- When being introduced, look the person in the eye. Say, "Hello" or "It's nice to meet you." Extend your hand as you respond vocally.

- When introducing people, use both the first and last names. Use Mr., Mrs., Dr., etc., in formal situations or in deference to age or position. Smile and speak distinctly. Add a bit of non-personal information about each person as a point of interest.

- Introduce yourself if there is no one to make the introduction.

- Never ask "remember me?" Reintroduce yourself.

1. **Age, gender, and hierarchy**
   - The younger person is introduced to the older person (e.g., Mr. Young, I would like you to meet Mrs. Elder).

   - Gender makes no difference. Historically the man has been introduced to the woman. Socially this still holds true, but in business, you needn't abide by this rule.

- Younger couples are introduced to older couples.

- In the business pecking order, introduce the junior to the senior (e.g., Ms. Junior, I would like to introduce you to Ms. Senior). When two people are of equal status, introduce the one you know less well to the one you know better.

- Introduce an untitled person to a titled person (e.g., Mr. Smith, I would like you to meet Lord Nelson).

- In a large group, introduce one person to a few people at a time.

2. **Complications**
- When you are being introduced, always remove your gloves except when wearing formal attire or in very cold weather.

- If your arms are full of files or parcels, don't try to juggle them to free your hand. Instead, nod your head as you respond.

- If someone forgets your name as he or she is introducing you, supply it quickly to save embarrassment.

- If you forget someone's name as you introduce him or her, say something light, like "computer breakdown, please excuse me." If the person doesn't supply his or her name, ask for it. (It's only really embarrassing when it's your boss or your mother!)

- If you have a name people have trouble saying or understanding, find something it rhymes with or something they can visualize.

- If you have been introduced before, allow yourself to be reintroduced if you are not recognized. Don't make an issue out of it.

3. Introducing a guest speaker

- Get background information on the person you are to introduce well beforehand. Check on how the speaker likes to be introduced. For example, if John Doe holds a Ph.D. does he prefer to be called Dr. Doe or Mr. Doe?

- Your introduction should give the speaker's name, credibility for speaking, and subject.

- Keep it short. An introduction should not exceed three minutes.

- Be enthusiastic. Make the audience want to hear the speaker, but don't tell them they will "learn something," "be greatly entertained," or to "listen carefully" or "pay attention."

- Don't read your introduction in a monotone. Use key word notes, and make eye contact with your audience.

- You can assure audience response by concluding your introduction with "Join me in a warm welcome for our speaker Jane Doe," and starting the applause.

GOOD MANNERS IN GOOD CONVERSATION

1. The basics

- Don't name drop.

- Don't constantly let people know where you've traveled.

- Don't ask about a person's age, weight, clothing size, religion, race, physical handicaps, financial affairs, price of clothing, jewelry, or other possessions.

- Don't discuss your personal problems, operations, or illnesses or those of others.

- Don't tell questionable, off-color, sexist, or racist jokes.

- Don't monopolize the conversation.

- If someone asks you questions you don't wish to answer, reply, "I don't know" or change the subject.

- Limit conversation during business hours.

2. **Initiating conversation**

A good conversationalist allows the other person to speak and participate. Try to make comments and ask questions that elicit response. Really listen.

- Focus on what the person is saying rather than your own thoughts.

- Nod, maintain eye contact. Interject short vocal cues like, "Then what happened?"

- Find a common interest, background, or situation to start with. The weather is ideal.

- If you want the conversation to continue, ask open-ended questions that allow the person to expand his or her thoughts.

- Ask close-ended questions, those that can be answered with "yes" or "no," or facts if you want to bring the conversation to a close.

- Use the person's name often.
- Don't be afraid to say "I don't know." Never try to "snow" someone.

3. **Polishing your act**

- Remember that business conversations can be overheard. Don't say anything that you don't want passed along in your business.
- Enunciate. Don't drop your "ings" at the end of words.
- Use good grammar, but don't correct anyone else's grammar.
- Don't use pompous, stuffy language.
- Don't fall in the habit of using outdated slang and cliches. You can get caught in a generation time lock.
- Accept compliments graciously with a thank you; don't protest or apologize.
- If you feel someone is giving wrong information, don't dispute it directly. You can say, instead, "But I thought...."

6
CULTURAL COURTESY

More and more business is being done in foreign countries as export and import markets grow and many businesses expand into multinationals. You won't get to first base in business if you don't observe the etiquette of the region. The more you read about the host country before you leave, the better.

It also shows respect and interest to be able to speak the language, even a few phrases. Before you leave on a trip, try to learn how to say please and thank you. Also helpful is learning to count to 10 and being able to introduce yourself. These simple phrases are not difficult in any language and can make the difference between a cordial or cool reception.

Also show appreciation for the different culture, music, and art. Be sensitive and nonjudgmental about the politics and religion, and, above all, learn to appreciate rather than depreciate.

SOME BASIC CONSIDERATIONS
It doesn't matter where you go, some rules of etiquette never change.

1. **General**
   - Respect the host company's dietary customs, holidays, religion, and government.
   - Don't make comparisons with your own country.
   - Don't criticize anything.
   - Business is more formal in all other cultures than in North America and may take more time.

39

- Always be punctual; traffic and crowds must be taken into consideration. (An exception to this rule is in Spain; the Spanish are less than punctual.)

- Don't flash large amounts of cash, and leave the family jewels at home.

- Don't make silly remarks about "funny money." Learn the monetary system of the country you are visiting.

- In many foreign countries the president of a company is called the managing director.

- Titles are very important. Use them.

- Correspondence should be very formal.

- If you visit a country on a continuing basis, have the reverse of your business card printed in the language of the country. Double check for accuracy.

- Profanity has no place in business, particularly international business where it is often considered not just bad manners but very offensive.

- Always stand for the national anthem of the country. Follow the actions of your host.

- Remember that you are not a tourist; leave your camera at home.

- Do not dress in native costumes such as togas or saris. You may find that you have chosen a garment that has specific religious cultural meaning.

- Do not demand that everything be as it is back home: showers, food, TV.

- Get names right. Memorize them. Work out complicated names phonetically. Names can denote family status and social rank. Do not call people by their given names unless asked to do so.

- Politeness counts in all countries, but particularly so in Asia.

2. Language

- If you don't speak the language of the country, hire an interpreter and learn some key phrases.

- If you speak the language, allow that you may not be as facile as your host.

- If you are speaking through an interpreter have another bilingual person on hand to monitor the translation and correct misinterpretation.

- You may politely ask your hosts to speak more slowly, placing the blame on your ability to understand. (Do not place the blame on them because they speak too fast.) Similarly, if you are conducting business in English, and you don't understand them, don't blame the other person's accent; blame your ear! Speak English slowly and articulate carefully.

- Don't try to tell any jokes; they usually are incomprehensible to people who speak other languages. Even other English-speaking people may not understand a play on words. For the same reason, don't use any slang.

3. Dress

- Good grooming is essential. Clothing should be inconspicuous, well-cut, and good quality. Dark suits and white shirts are expected. Women

41

should not wear pants, overly short skirts, or sleeveless dresses.

- Avoid drip-dry materials. They are the mark of a tourist.

- Shoes are forbidden in Buddhist temples, Muslim mosques, Japanese homes and restaurants, and Indian and Indonesian homes. Place them neatly together, facing the door.

4. **Travel**

- Arrive early at airports for security checks. In some countries two hours are necessary for this purpose.

- Have all your documentation easily at hand.

- Be prepared to leave your passport at hotels while staying in some countries.

5. **Paying your way**

- It is inconsiderate to waste water, heat, and light in other countries.

- In some countries, telephones are metered. Don't make calls without offering to pay.

- Tipping is generally done on the same basis as at home (except in Italy and South America where a 20% tip is expected and in Egypt where tipping is heavy). If the gratuity is already added, you may leave a small tip for special service. When using a credit card, leave the tip in cash. Tipping is discouraged in the Commonwealth of Independent States (formerly the U.S.S.R.), New Zealand, and Islamic countries. In the Commonwealth of Independent States and Japan, use cash. In Japan, place cash in the envelope when the bill comes. (See the following section on etiquette in various countries.)

- Small, easily packed, useful but inexpensive gifts are appreciated by hotel and restaurant personnel. They don't replace a tip, but can be given for appreciation of special service.

6. Handshakes

- Shaking hands is important in Europe and shouldn't be neglected when meeting or greeting someone.

- Wait for women to extend their hands, for in some countries women still do not shake hands.

- Expect to be kissed on the cheeks in France and Mediterranean countries and embraced in Latin countries. In India, you press your own palms together in greeting.

7. Smoking

In most other nations, most adults smoke. Non-smoking rules are unheard of. The exception is in Islamic countries which are non-smoking. Don't press your non-smoking ethic on your hosts.

8. Age and gender

- Show respect for the elderly. Wait until they extend their hands in greeting.

- Stand when an elderly person enters the room. Allow him or her to speak first.

- In many countries, women still do not take part in business. Where they do, social manners, not modern, North American business manners, are expected.

9. Food	• Eat what you are offered. Don't ask what it is. Cut it up into small bites and it goes down easily!
10. Religion	• Avoid as a topic for discussion. Learn as much as you can about the religion of the region. Religion has a very strong influence on business in many countries: hours of business, months of business. Religious artifacts may be part of the furnishings. Remember, Buddhist images are holy: never step on a door sill in Thailand (kindly spirits dwell below), do not interrupt anyone facing Mecca, do not photograph or touch religious objects without permission.
11. Business cards	• Business cards are a must. They should include your company name, your position, plus any titles (e.g., manager, director). Do not use abbreviations.
	• As mentioned before, have one side printed in the local language. (Overnight service is available in Hong Kong and Tokyo.) Have it checked to make sure the translation is correct.
	• In Southeast Asia, Africa, and the Middle East, always present your card with the right hand.
	• In Japan present your card with both hands, right side up, type facing the recipient.
12. Gestures	• The circled thumb and forefinger, the V for victory sign, and the "thumbs up" signal all have very different meanings in other countries. President Bush shocked the usually

unshockable Australians because his jubilant victory sign was actually a very vulgar expression. Like slang, gestures should be avoided.

CULTURAL DIFFERENCES

Here are some of the specific differences to watch out for when doing business in foreign countries.

1. Africa
- North African countries follow Arabic or Muslim customs. The middle nations are black multi-cultures and South Africa is a mixture of Dutch, English, and African tribes.

- English is spoken in most countries, but you'll find the language of previous occupation dominant in others: French in Ivory Coast.

- Avoid political discussion, particularly in reference to previously occupying countries.

2. Arab countries
- Food and drink is often consumed before business. Even if you aren't hungry, don't refuse. Eat what you can.

- Wear a light-weight dark suit, shirt, and tie. No slacks for women. All extremities should be covered.

- Use your right hand. The left hand is used only for very personal hygiene. Apologize if you are left-handed.

- Don't point at or beckon a person.

- Arabs stand very close in conversation. Do not step back.

- Do not enquire about an Arab's family; private life is not discussed.

- Keep your feet on the floor. Do not expose the soles of your feet.

- Do not tease, argue, or in any way hurt your host's pride.

3. **Australia**

- Because of the climate, dress in the Australian business world is casual. In the summer, men often wear long shorts with executive-length socks, a shirt, and a tie.

- Business is male dominated.

- Business is very democratic.

4. **Austria**

- Be punctual.

- Do not refer to Austrians as Germans.

- Very formal. No first names.

- Shake hands firmly and make strong and use direct eye contact.

- Keep both hands on the table when eating.

5. **Belgium**

- Private, formal people with a good sense of humor.

- Very punctual.

- Putting your hands in your pockets is impolite.

- Do not confuse with the French.

6. **Bulgaria**

- Few English speaking.

- A nod means no. Shaking the head means yes.

- Very punctual.

- Appointments must be made well in advance and confirmed in writing.

- Much hand shaking.

7. **Caribbean**
- The Caribbean consists of independent countries and territories. Some have been influenced by the Spanish, others by the Dutch, English, and French.
- In general, the handshake is common.
- There is a more relaxed pace of doing business. The exception is Puerto Rico which can sometimes seem like New York.
- Business cards are important.
- Punctuality is not so important.

8. **China (People's Republic of)**
- Don't get down to business immediately. Let the interpreters guide the way.
- Don't make any body contact — no hugs, kisses, or touching.
- Use a quiet voice and demeanor.
- Remember, the family name comes first: Fung Lee is Mr. Fung.
- Exchange business cards on meeting.
- Learn to enjoy tea. It will be served often during business hours.
- Dress very conservatively.
- Do not wear white.
- Rather than displease you with the truth, the Chinese may avoid it. Don't apply pressure or be upset.

9. **Commonwealth of Independent States (formerly U.S.S.R.)**
- Check and double check who you are to see and where you are to see them. Get all information in writing. Daily changes are part of the new freedom.

- Confirm in writing.

- Be punctual.

- Be sure of where you are! Former states now have become independent countries and must be recognized as such.

- When you meet someone, shake hands and give your name. Don't be surprised if you are greeted with a bear hug when meeting someone repeatedly.

10. Czechoslovakia
- Two languages: Czech and Slovak.

- Make appointments well in advance.

- Very punctual.

- Much handshaking.

11. Denmark
- Very punctual.

- Firm handshaking, even with children.

- Don't confuse with Swedes or Norwegians.

- If asked to dinner, you will be expected to make a toast. (Dinners are long with many toasts.)

12. Egypt
- Be prepared to wait...and wait.

- Business vacations are taken from June to September (Ramadan is observed).

- Prior appointments are necessary.

- Dress conservatively.

- Shake hands with everyone in the office.

- Have business cards printed in both English and Arabic.

13. England
- Address people formally (i.e., Mr., Mrs., Ms.)
- Keep physical contact to the minimum.
- Take your umbrella (black).
- Working days are 9 a.m. to 5 p.m.
- Get used to common expressions and don't find them "funny."
- Don't ask any personal questions or initiate personal discussions.
- Show respect for the royal family.
- Dress formally.

14. France
- Address people formally.
- The business day is 8:30 a.m. to 12:30 p.m.; 3:00 p.m. to 6:30 p.m. The French go home for lunch. The farther south you travel, the less strictly you will find they adhere to the clock.
- There are never breakfast meetings.
- Handshakes on arrival and departure are very important.
- Always confirm your meeting in writing and with very correct French.
- Don't use any high pressure tactics.

15. Germany
- Don't put your hands in your pockets.
- Handshakes should be firm.
- Rank is important in meetings.
- Keep both hands on the table when eating.

- Executives are often addressed by their profession or position.
- Business is very formal and cautious.
- Make appointments well in advance.
- Be punctual.
- Don't make small talk; business is business.

16. Greece
- Food and drink are often served before business.
- Business is very formal and very male dominated.
- Use social manners toward women.
- There are no business lunches. Eating is a social experience.
- Do not use the thumb and forefinger signal for "okay" (which is very obscene in Greece).

17. Hong Kong
- Business is done every day and every hour of the day and often conducted in restaurants.
- Most business people speak English.
- Business cards are essential.
- Make prior appointments and be punctual.
- Women are accepted as equals.
- Do not dress in white or royal blue; these colors represent mourning.
- Shake hands in greeting; generally follow other British customs.
- Winking or beckoning with the index finger is rude.
- It is a non-touching society.

18. Hungary
- Handshakes all round.

- Very polite and formal.
- Self-deprecating if you compliment them or their work.

19. India
- Men shake hands. When you greet a woman, put palms together and bow slightly.
- Great respect for the elderly.
- Hindus do not eat beef. The cow is sacred.
- Pass food with your right hand.
- Use British business manners.

20. Indonesia
- Business hours are 8:00 a.m. to 3:00 p.m. Monday to Thursday.
- Don't use your left hand to give or receive anything.
- Don't crook your finger to call someone.
- Loud voices are offensive.

21. Israel
- Don't waste time.
- Dress is very informal. Shorts, shirts, and shirt-sleeves are acceptable; men needn't wear ties.
- "Shalom" is used in business as a greeting for hello and goodbye.
- The work week begins on Sunday morning.

22. Italy
- Address people formally.
- The working day is 9:00 a.m. to 1:00 p.m.; 4:00 p.m. to 8:00 p.m.
- Use titles of profession and position.
- Handshakes are very important.

23. Japan

- In Japan, business always takes precedence. Hours include dinner.

- Business is very male dominated.

- Business may begin with a tea ceremony. Take part.

- Be very formal. Do not chat with receptionists or secretaries.

- Be punctual.

- Don't maintain strong eye contact. Be "humble."

- Do not make body contact with the other person, and do not crowd the person you are talking to by standing too close.

- Handshaking is not widely used as a greeting. Bow only if someone bows to you. Bow from the waist, lowering your head about one foot with your hands together. When given a gift, say thank you and bow. The more important or older the person is that you are bowing to, the deeper the bow.

- Keep your voice and gestures subdued.

- Shoes are not removed at places of business. Be prepared to remove shoes at restaurants and homes.

- Confirm your meeting in writing and send the agenda in advance.

- Gifts are expected. Appropriate is something representative of your country and in good taste. Gifts are not opened in front of the giver.

- Acknowledge any gift given you immediately and in writing.

- Take a lot of business cards, but bring them out at the beginning of a business conversation, not at the end. It is considered impolite to keep your business cards in your pants pocket; instead, keep a supply in your jacket.

- Be prepared to be treated with great deference by younger or junior staff. Even senior or older executives will defer to you because you are a guest.

- In polite conversation, the suffix "san" is added to the surname in place of Mr., Mrs., or Ms. (e.g., Suzuki-san)

24. Latin America

- The siesta is still observed in many countries and business can go on late at night.

- Dress is very formal.

- Don't be overly concerned about time.

- Handshakes and embraces are frequent.

- Women rarely take part in business; they must be treated with social respect.

- "No" may mean "perhaps." Don't give up.

25. Netherlands

- Prior appointments are necessary.

- Dress conservatively.

- Business vacations are taken during June to August.

- Do not refer to The Netherlands as Holland. (Holland is just a small part of The Netherlands.)

- Dutch is a generic term and should not be used. Use Netherlanders.

- Do not be surprised if you are offered a drink during business hours. Don't refuse. Drink some of it.

26. Norway

- Be very punctual.

- Do not confuse with Danes and Swedes.

- Formal in address. May call you by your last name.

27. Persian Gulf countries

- No business is done during Ramadan (the ninth month of the Mohammedan year observed as sacred with fasting practiced daily from dawn to sunset) and other holy days.

- No business is conducted from Thursday night to Friday night, which is the Sabbath.

- Dress is formal. Wear dark clothing and cover all your limbs. Women should not wear slacks.

- Be prepared to drink mint tea and sweet black coffee. Food and drink should never be refused.

- Women do not take part in business.

- Be patient. Don't try to hurry the process.

28. Philippines

- Do not be late for business, but be 30 minutes late for dinner so as not to appear over-eager.

- Address your business associate by occupational title.

- Business hours are 9:00 a.m. to 5:00 p.m. (sometimes 5:30 p.m.)

29. Poland
- Use formal greetings and handshakes.
- Poles are very proud of history and culture, but former associations with U.S.S.R. and Germany are topics to avoid.

30. Portugal
- Men embrace in greeting.
- Be prompt.
- You can discuss business over lunch but not over dinner.
- Do not confuse with Spain in any way.

31. Romania
- Very punctual.
- Much handshaking.
- Formal in address.

32. Saudi Arabia
- No liquor is allowed in the country. Under no circumstances should you try to bring in any alcohol. The penalties are severe.
- Don't smoke unless your host does.
- Women do not dine with men even at a business dinner.

33. Singapore
- Be punctual.
- English is the language of business.
- Practical and straight to the point; expect blunt questions.
- Women are treated as equals in business.
- Shake hands in greeting and present your business card with both hands.
- Business hours are 9:00 a.m. to 5:00 p.m. for government; 10:00 a.m. to 6:00 p.m. for stores.

- Smoking in public, jay walking, and littering are all prohibited.
- Long hair is disapproved of.

34. South Korea
- Men bow and shake hands. Women do not shake hands.
- Avoid direct eye contact.
- Open mouth is rude. Be sure to cover it when you laugh.
- Don't blow your nose in public.
- Show respect for elderly, humility and patience.

35. Spain
- Business is very formal
- Business status is strictly adhered to.
- Time and punctuality are not adhered to.
- Men greet men with an abrazo (hug).
- The main meal is from 1:30 to 4:30 p.m. Business continues from 6:00 p.m. to 10:00 p.m. (The Spanish thrive on very little sleep!)

36. Sweden
- Don't confuse with Norwegians and Danes.
- Be punctual.
- Swedes may appear stiff and serious until you get to know them.
- Don't be overly confident. No bragging.
- Don't expect compliments.

37. Switzerland
- Be very punctual.
- Respect courtesy and good manners.
- The Swiss tend to be very conservative and don't like ostentatious display of personal worth.

	• English is the language of business.
38. Taiwan	• Very friendly. Most speak English.
	• Close friendships valued in business.
	• Gift giving common. Gifts can be expensive.
	• Business cards are essential and should be printed in English and Chinese. Present and receive cards in both hands.
	• Never touch anyone on the head.
	• Do not point with one finger.
	• Be punctual.
	• Do not confuse with Hong Kong or mainland China; within the country, refer to it as the Republic of China.
39. Yugoslavia	• Usually punctual.
	• Shake hands firmly and often.
	• Expect tea, coffee, even a snack.
	• May ask more personal questions than other European countries.

BUSINESS DINNERS ABROAD

1. China (People's Republic of)	• Arrive promptly, but leave very soon after the meal if you are the guest of honor. No one can leave until the guest of honor leaves.
	• Your host will most likely toast you early in the meal. Wait, and return the toast.
	• If a banquet is given in your honor, you must give one in return and of equal quality.
	• Tipping is prohibited.

- Thanks are expected. If you can have your thank you note to the hotel or restaurant manager written in Chinese, it will assure that you will always be welcome.

2. **France**
- If you invite someone out to a business dinner, choose an excellent restaurant. (Excellent translates as expensive.)
- Allow your guest to choose the wine if you are unsure. Praise the choice. Wine is important to the French.
- Beer may be served at room temperature.
- Salad is served after the main course.
- Don't expect the bill to be put on the table as soon as you are finished dessert; dining is very leisurely and you will have to ask for the bill.

3. **Germany**
- You may very often attend a concert as well as dinner. Be prepared for a formal evening.

4. **Greece**
- Some cafes are for men only.
- Food may be served at room temperature.
- Dish smashing takes place in special bars and can be an expensive diversion.

5. **Hong Kong**
- Don't be surprised when rice bowls are held close to the mouth and food is eaten with more noise than you are used to.

6. **Islamic countries**
- Choose a large hotel with an international menu.

- No alcohol is served.

- Pork is never eaten.

- Never refuse any food or drink offered. Eat or drink little.

7. **Israel**
- Most restaurants are kosher. Shellfish and pork are not served. Dairy and meat products are not mixed on the same plates.

8. **Italy**
- Coffee is served black.

- Pasta and soup are both appetizers. Choose one.

- Salad is served after the main course.

- Some cafes are for men only.

9. **Japan**
- If you are male, don't bring your wife.

- Geishas still serve in many restaurants.

- Leave your shoes inside the door. They should be facing outward. Then it is correct to put on the house slippers provided.

- Don't step on the door sill or, when you are seated for dinner, point your feet at another guest. Instead, tuck your feet under or to the side.

- When you use the bathroom, take off your house slippers and slip on the pair outside the bathroom door left for that use.

- Food is accompanied by extensive drinking and is very expensive. But never pour your own sake (Japanese wine); it is usual to pour for other guests and allow them to fill yours.

- Never leave chopsticks in a bowl. Never leave chopsticks crossed. Place them side by side on the rest provided.

- Chopsticks are held in your right hand if you are right-handed. Your soup or rice bowl is held in the left. Don't put your thumb in your rice or soup bowl. Chopsticks are like forks and spoons; they shouldn't be waved in the air while you are talking or stuck in your food. Learn how to use them correctly.

- Host and hostess sit together at one end of the table. The honored guest sits in front of an alcove.

- A 10% service charge will be automatically added to the bill. If you wish to leave more, place it in an envelope and give it to the head waiter discreetly.

10. Latin America
- Dinner will begin late.
- Don't smoke at the table.

11. Scandinavia
- Be punctual.
- Men should wear suits; women should wear dinner dresses.
- The honored guest sits on host's left.
- Be prepared to toast and be toasted.

INVITATIONS TO PRIVATE HOMES
- If you are asked to a home, accept. If possible, send flowers before your arrival. Bring expensive candy for adults and treats for the children in countries where the family life is strong. (In Scandinavia, take flowers or expensive chocolates.) Do not take wine or alcohol.

- Always compliment your hosts on their home. If children are present, compliment your hosts on their children, but do not pat children on the head. Compliment the food and the hostess who cooked it.

7
TABLE MANNERS

We are all judged by our table manners. Unfortunately, many otherwise qualified business people have very poor table manners. Many people who are now in management positions were brought up in the sixties when there was less emphasis on "very proper" behavior and formal banquets were less common. Now, these same people are often in the position of attending business functions that include all styles of dining and they don't know which fork to use or where to begin. Or worse, they unknowingly make errors.

Whether you like it or not, your table manners can make the difference between getting that promotion or not, closing that business deal or not. Fortunately, old habits can be changed — if you want to change them — but it takes effort.

THE BASICS (OR — WHAT YOU SHOULD HAVE LEARNED AT HOME)

1. Eating

- Don't begin to eat until your host begins or indicates you should do so.

- Don't chew with your mouth open.

- Don't talk with food in your mouth.

- Don't fill your mouth so full that chewing and swallowing become an effort.

- Chew thoroughly and swallow all food before putting more in your mouth or before taking a drink.

- Don't spit seeds, pits, etc., into your palm. As it went in, so it should come out! The exception can be fish bones, which should be removed as inconspicuously as possible with your thumb and forefinger and placed on your bread and butter plate.

- Don't mash or mix food on your plate.

- Don't dunk — not even doughnuts!

- Break bread and buns. Never use your knife.

- Break off a small piece of bread or bun and butter it. Don't butter the whole slice or half a bun at one time.

- If you wish to share food — use your bread plate.

- Don't blow on hot food or drink.

- Don't sip from a coffee spoon or teaspoon.

- Soup should be spooned away from you. Tilt the bowl away from you. Don't crumble crackers into your soup. They are to be eaten with the soup. The exception: oyster crackers. (Sorry! All of you who crunch up crackers in the cellophane and dump them in your soup have to stop. Do it at home — alone.)

- Only clear consomme should be drunk, and only if the soup bowl has handles.

- You may use a piece of bread on a fork to soak up sauce or gravy. Never hold the bread in your fingers and do this.

- You may eat chicken and pizza with your fingers if you are at a barbecue or very informal setting. Otherwise use a knife and fork for chicken.

2. Napkins, dishes, and cutlery

- Your napkin should be placed on your lap. A small napkin may be opened fully. A large dinner napkin should be kept folded in half with the fold toward you. Don't tuck your napkin into the collar of your shirt.

- In some restaurants the waiter will place your napkin on your lap for you. You can be prepared by observation.

- The host leads off in placing the napkin. Follow the lead.

- When you are finished dining, place your napkin in loose folds at the left side of your plate, never on top of the plate. Keep your napkin in your lap until you leave the table.

- Never use a napkin as a handkerchief.

- Don't wipe off cutlery or glassware with your napkin. If dishes aren't clean, ask the waiter quietly for replacements.

- Soup spoons, coffee spoons, and dessert spoons should be placed on the service plate or saucer when you are finished eating. Never leave them in the bowl, cup, or parfait glass.

- Don't wave cutlery when you talk.

- Don't draw on the table cloth with anything, including utensils.

- Don't scrape the pattern off the plate.

- Never use your fingers to push food into your spoon or fork.

- When you are finished eating, don't push your plate away or stack your dishes. Place your knife and fork together in the "twenty past four" position, as if your plate were the face of the clock, with the knife on the outside and the fork on the inside. Or place the utensils side by side in the middle of your plate, fork tines down, knife to the right, sharp blade turned inward toward the fork.

3. Passing dishes and food

- Never reach! If the food isn't directly in front of you, ask for it to be passed.

- Initiate the passing of buns, butter, and condiments even if you do not wish any. Pass to the right.

- Pass pitchers, gravy boats etc. with the handle toward the recipient.

4. Posture and presence

- Keep all "uncooked joints off the table." Elbows should not be on the table until after all courses have been cleared away and you are engaged in after-dinner conversation. Don't lean on your elbows! Keep your posture erect.

- Don't tilt back in your chair.

- Don't belch! Cover your mouth with your napkin. After it happens, say a quiet "pardon me" to no one in particular.

- If you spill on the table, yourself, or someone else, discreetly use your napkin or ask the waiter for seltzer water. Do not dip your napkin into your water glass. Let victims of your indiscretion blot for themselves. Offer to cover any laundering or cleaning costs.

- If you break anything, call it to the waiter's attention. In a private home, speak quietly to the host and offer to replace. Do not turn the incident into a catastrophe.

- Don't use toothpicks, fingernails, or napkins to dislodge food. If you're in agony, retire to the bathroom and take care of it.

- Don't smoke during a meal. Smoking should not take place until dessert is finished. Follow the lead of the host or ask if you may smoke. Use ashtrays only.

- Don't crook your little finger; it is a parody on good manners.

- Don't apply makeup or comb your hair at the table.

- When you wish to use the washroom, excuse yourself and leave quietly. Don't ask people where they are going if they excuse themselves.

EATING STYLES

There are two different, acceptable eating styles in North America. The first, the American style, is used by many in the United States and by some in Canada. With this style, when cutting food, the fork is held in the left hand and the knife in the right hand. Then the knife is put down and the fork exchanged, from the left to the right hand to put food on the fork and into the mouth.

The continental style is used throughout the world, including Canada and by some people in the United States. Some people consider this the more acceptable style. The fork is held in the left hand, the knife in the right to cut food and to help carry food to the fork. The fork is held, tines down, and the knife used to move food unto the fork or support food so the fork can pick it up. There is no shifting of utensils.

- Whatever style you use, do not cut up more than three bites at a time.

- Don't make a fist around your fork or knife.

- Don't hold the fork perpendicular to the food and saw with your knife.

THE FORMAL TABLE SETTING

At first glance, a formal table setting can be intimidating because there are numerous forks, spoons, and knives, all for different courses. However, don't be dismayed, there is a simple system behind it all. (See Figure #3.)

1. **Placement and procedure**

- Start with the utensils on the outside and work your way inward with each subsequent course. In other words, the outermost fork is your salad fork if salad is served first.

- Forks will be on your left. Knives and spoons on your right. One exception to this is the oyster or seafood fork, which will be on the right next to the soup spoon.

- If you do not order fish, soup, or salad, the waiter will remove those utensils. In a private home or at a banquet the silverware indicates the courses that will be served.

- At the top of your plate will be a dessert spoon and dessert fork. When dessert is served, slide them down to the sides of the dessert plate: fork on the left; spoon on the right.

- To eat dessert, break the dessert with the spoon, one bite at a time. Push the food with the fork into the spoon. Eat from the spoon. (Fork in left hand; spoon in right.)

- Coffee spoons are either to the right of the plate or brought with the coffee.

- Red wine is served in a glass with a round bowl and fairly short stem. Hold it at the base of the bowl. It will be served at room temperature. White wine is served in a larger glass with a longer stem. Hold it at the base of the stem. The same applies to all chilled wines. The order of the wine glasses begins with the one closest to you:

  (a) Sherry (soup course)

  (b) White wine (fish/chicken course)

  (c) Red wine (meat course)

  (d) Water goblet

There may be other glasses used throughout the meal; see Figure #4.

- There will be a butter knife located near the butter dish. Use it to transfer butter to your side plate. Your butter knife will either be lying diagonally across your side plate or as the last one to your right in the row of knives. Never use the knife with the butter dish to butter bread. If there is no knife with the butter dish, transfer the butter with your butter knife.

- Sorbet, a fruit flavored ice, may be served between courses to cleanse the palate. A spoon will accompany the sorbet.

- Salad may be served before or after the main course. The placement of the salad fork will give you a clue.

- Finger bowls are presented after the main course and before dessert. If the bowl is placed on a plate directly in front of you, lift the bowl with both hands and place it to the left of your place setting. If there is a doily under it, move it as well. Often the finger bowl will be placed to the left. Dip the fingers of one hand into the bowl, dry on your napkin which remains on you lap. Follow with the other hand. There may be a flower or a lemon slice in the bowl. Leave it be. (Some restaurants use hot towels in a similar manner as finger bowl.

2. **Seating at a formal dinner**
   - Learn the rules for formal dinners. (See Figure #5 for a seating plan.)
   - The male guest of honor sits on the hostess' right.
   - The next most important man sits on her left.
   - The female guest of honor sits on the host's right.
   - The second most important woman sits on the host's left.
   - Men and women should be alternately seated.
   - Couples should be separated.
   - Use of round tables puts everyone on an equal basis.
   - There may be place cards at a formal dinner or your host/hostess may indicate where you should be seated.
   - Social manners are expected: males should seat females and rise when they leave and return to the table.

FIGURE #3
THE FORMAL TABLE SETTING

1. Sherry glass
2. White wine glass
3. Red wine glass
4. Water goblet
5. Seafood fork
6. Soup spoon
7. Dinner knife
8. Dinner fork
9. Salad fork
10. Dessert fork and spoon
11. Butter plate

FIGURE #4
TYPES OF GLASSES

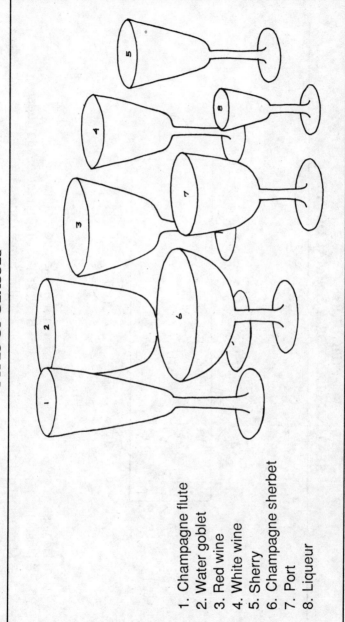

1. Champagne flute
2. Water goblet
3. Red wine
4. White wine
5. Sherry
6. Champagne sherbet
7. Port
8. Liqueur

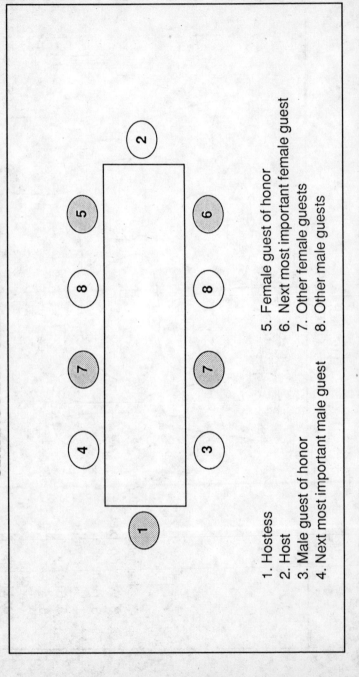

FIGURE #5
SEATING PLAN FOR A FORMAL DINNER

1. Hostess
2. Host
3. Male guest of honor
4. Next most important male guest
5. Female guest of honor
6. Next most important female guest
7. Other female guests
8. Other male guests

DRESS

There's nothing worse than discovering you've dressed incorrectly for a function. If you receive an invitation that gives no indication of dress requirements, telephone your host and ask. The following will guide you on formal wear.

1. **Semi-formal**

   (a) Men
   - Good quality dark suit
   - White shirt, dark tie
   - Dark socks and black shoes

   (b) Women
   - Ballet or cocktail-length dress

2. **Formal**

   (a) Men
   - Tuxedo preferred
   - Dark suit acceptable in some situations. Enquire.
   - Do not wear tails.

   (b) Women
   - Long dress

3. **Black tie**

   (a) Men
   - Tuxedo (dinner jacket)
   - White dress shirt, cuff links and studs
   - Cummerbund
   - Black silk socks
   - Black patent leather shoes

(b) Women

- Long dress

- Sheer hose

- Peau-de-soie pumps (i.e., heavy silk or silk-like material) dyed to match dress or evening sandals

4. **White tie**

(a) Men

- Tails

- White wing shirt, cuff links and studs

- White bow tie

- White cummerbund or white vest

- White gloves (optional)

(b) Women

- Long dress

- Sheer hose

- Peau-de-soie pumps dyed to match dress or evening sandals

- Long, white gloves

Play it safe. Colorful ties and cummerbunds are not businesslike. Low-cut, slinky, sexy dresses are not suitable for business functions. Good taste and decorum are essential to your reputation.

R.S.V.P.

The greatest single modern business (and social) etiquette failing is not responding to an invitation to let the host know whether or not you will attend. Respond before the date given on the invitation.

8

EATING IN AND DINING OUT

Food and business have always been boon companions, but the day of the three-hour, three-martini business lunch is gone and for good reason. No one can function properly or make wise decisions with that much booze under the belt, and the tax department casts a jaundiced eye at such expense accounts.

Today's rationale for food and business is time. There just aren't enough hours in the day to complete all business unless you include breakfast, lunch, and dinner. Keeping that in mind, let's start with some basics:

- Always keep to time. Busy people have tight schedules.

- Order items that can be eaten easily. No one wants to spend the rest of the day with reminders of spaghetti on a blouse or tie.

- Watch the booze. Business and booze don't mix. Business dining means business will be conducted.

- If you are invited out, not only you but your spouse or companion are under scrutiny. Many good employees have not made it to the top floor because of poor manners and decorum. Companies don't like to take chances. (See chapter 7 for more on table manners.)

- Be considerate of your guests. Determine if they are non-smokers,

75

vegetarians, or on a special diet before making reservations.

DINING OUT

1. Choosing the restaurant

- Keep in mind the different styles of restaurants. "Table d'hote" means everything is a set price which includes soup or salad, a main course (entree), dessert, and tea or coffee. It doesn't include appetizer or wine. "A la carte" means all items are individually priced.

- If possible choose a restaurant you know. If you must choose a restaurant with which you are unfamiliar, check it out personally before you make reservations. Ask for the price range of entrees and hours of service. Check out closeness of tables, cleanliness, and type of background music played.

- Choose a location close to your guest's office or central to both of you.

- Never ask your guest where he or she would like to eat, but give your guest a choice of two places.

2. Small talk — the warm up

- Small talk should never get into ethnic or religious subjects unless you know you have the same background. Politics is a safe subject only as related to office business or if you know you and your guest have the same political preference. Never discuss sex or personal problems; never gossip or tell questionable jokes; never ask anyone how much they earn or how much they paid for any-thing.

- Safe subjects are the weather, sports, state of the economy, common inter-ests, and common acquaintances.

3. **Paying the bill**
- The bill is always paid by the person who did the inviting.

- If a restaurant is new to you, take the maitre d' aside and ask him to be sure the bill is brought to you. If you are a woman, this is especially im-portant, since many waiters still present the bill to the male, creating a moment of embarrassment at the end of the meal. A waiter should know that the person who orders the wine or asks for the bill is the host.

- If you eat regularly at a restaurant, you may arrange to have yourself billed monthly and just sign for the bill.

- You may make arrangements for the tip and bill with the maitre d' before-hand, using your credit card so all you have to do is sign at the end of the meal.

- Use a credit card when paying. Cold cash seems crass. Cash may be used in cafeterias and fast food outlets.

- Check the bill for accuracy and cal-culate the tip quickly. Don't make it an elaborate production. If there is an error, speak quietly to the waiter.

- Don't arm wrestle over the bill. If someone has such poor manners as to insist on paying, let it be.

77

4. Tipping
- For good food and good service, tip 15% of the bill excluding any tax.

- For excellent food and service, tip 20% — no more.

- The captain, maitre d', or sommelier (wine captain) tips are computed at 7% of the untaxed bill or one-half of the waiter's tip.

- All tips (excluding cloakroom) should be left at the table, given directly to the person, or put on the credit card.

- Cloakroom tips range from 25¢ to $1 per person and are left at the point of checking.

- If service has been inexcusably bad, with no apologies, you may show you do not accept such treatment by not leaving a tip. Let the manager know that service was unacceptable and that you did not tip.

5. Emergencies
- Should your guest experience a sudden illness or choking, the meal is automatically ended. Pay the bill and slip the waiter and maitre d' extra money to show your appreciation for their help.

- Nose bleeds, coughing, or sneezing can be handled by excusing yourself to the washroom. Return to the table when you are composed.

- If your dining companion does not return from the washroom within a short time, you should enquire as to his or her well-being.

- If a person becomes ill during lunch, call the next day to enquire after him or her.

6. **The unexpected**
- If smoking, loud music, raucous laughter, rudeness, or drunkenness interfere with your dining, speak to your waiter to ask the maitre d' or manager to handle it. Don't speak to the offenders yourself.

- If nothing is done, leave, expressing your dissatisfaction to the manager, coolly and calmly. Apologize to your guests as you leave the restaurant. Thank your guests for their patience.

- If a guest acts in a boorish manner, end the meal as quickly as possible.

- If a host acts in a boorish manner, discover you had forgotten an appointment and bring the meal to a close as quickly as possible.

- If strangers are listening in on your conversation, stop in mid-sentence and stare intently at them until they turn away and mind their own business.

- If a friend or business associate is listening, change the subject; speak in lower tones or adjourn to more private surroundings.

THE BUSINESS BREAKFAST

Breakfast can be the best time of day to do business, but keep in mind that not everyone is an early bird. Breakfast meetings are most effective with out-of-town visitors, with someone whom you want an immediate decision from, when your agenda is short, or when your time is limited.

- Arrange to meet at a time and place convenient for your guest.

- Reservations may not be possible, so arrive early, secure a table, and let the maitre d' know you are expecting someone. (Let your guest know you will be waiting at your table.)

- Stand up fully or partially when your guest arrives. (Booths make this difficult.)

- See that your guest is served coffee immediately and the orders taken as soon as possible. (Select a restaurant or coffee shop because of the good service. Food can be secondary at this time of day.)

- Get down to business. The food and the talk should come to a successful conclusion at the same time.

- The host pays. Cash may be quicker than a credit card and is acceptable as the amount will not be great.

- A vocal thank you only is expected.

THE BUSINESS LUNCH

Invite someone to a business lunch when you have a good reason to do so. State your reason when issuing the invitation, and speak directly to the person, not to the secretary. Some people consider lunches less formal and, therefore, less important. Keep in mind that everyone is busy: cancel only when absolutely necessary.

1. **Lunching with a guest**
   - The person who cancels should reschedule as soon as possible. However, the original host remains the host and pays the bill.
   - Make the reservation in your full name.

- If you are hosting, arrive a few minutes early. If you are the guest, be on time.

- Pay for checking your guest's coat.

- Be sure your guest is seated in the preferred seat — where the occupant looks out onto the restaurant.

- As host, feel free to suggest or recommend something from the menu. You should order first, setting an example for price for the guest.

- Do not let the whole meal become small talk. Get down to business before the dessert or your time will be gone.

- The host picks up all the costs of everything charged for in the restaurant. This includes all the drinks, even if your guest arrived early and had a drink at the bar, and whatever fee or tip is required at the coat-check room. If the guest is holding his or her coat check tag, ask for it after the meal and then present both your's and your guest's to the person at the coat room.

- The host's obligation ends outside the door of the restaurant.

- The guest should send a short typewritten thank you.

2. Lunching with co-workers

- When lunching with co-workers, each pays for what he or she ordered. If possible, ask for separate bills. If co-workers earn equal incomes, they can split the bill evenly.

- If someone hasn't had any drinks, split the food bill; then the drinkers can add the bar bill and pay the difference.

THE BUSINESS COCKTAIL PARTY

1. **For guests**
   - Mingle. Talk to as many people as possible but do not force yourself into an intense conversation.
   - Hosts should introduce guests to one another, but introduce yourself if there is no one to make introductions. Be aware of others on their own and include them in your conversation group.
   - Limit your drinking and don't use any drugs.
   - Limit your eating. Don't make the hors d'oeuvres substitute for dinner.
   - You may have to use your napkin as a plate. Select food that is the least messy.
   - Limit your smoking. If there are designated areas, use them. Use ashtrays.
   - Don't overstay. Leave before the designated time on your invitation.
   - Send a typewritten thank you to your host.

2. **For hosts**
   - See that people are meeting and talking. Introduce your guests to each other, and watch for anyone who is being left alone.
   - Make sure that food and drinks are replenished.
   - Feel free to shut down the bar at a designated time.

- To indicate the party is over, position yourself at the door to see guests out.

EATING IN THE OFFICE

1. **At your desk**
   - If you "brown bag" lunch or pick it up at the cafeteria, eat at your desk only when pressed for time. Eat at your designated lunch time. Do not eat at your desk on office time because you went jogging or shopping over the lunch hour.

   - Clear your desk before eating. Ketchup stains on the spread sheet don't "cut the mustard" with management.

   - Clean up afterward — that includes your desk and yourself.

2. **At meetings**
   - Eat at meetings only if food is provided or you are asked to bring your lunch.

   - Do not bring your lunch to a meeting or seminar called before or after the designated breakfast or lunch hour. No one wants to watch or listen to people munch and crunch because they caught a late bus or looked at new cars through their lunch hour.

   - Pass the food and then get down to business or vice versa. Serving food at a meeting is meant to save time, but often time is wasted because the focus is on the food and not on the agenda.

   - Be considerate of passing and taking. Someone else might like one of the shrimp sandwiches, so don't load four on your plate.

- Do not talk with your mouth full.

3. The business cafeteria

There are times when guests eat in the company cafeteria; there are times when you will eat in the cafeteria alone. Both situations call for good manners.

- Explain to a guest how the cafeteria works and what is available.

- Let your guest follow you.

- Don't hold up the line. Read the specials board and have a good idea about what you want before getting in line.

- Be courteous and considerate to cafeteria employees.

- Don't force yourself on others, especially senior management.

- Invite others to join you if you wish company. It's a good way to get to know other employees.

- If you are lunching with a business guest and someone asks to join you, graciously let him or her know that you are doing business, but that you would be glad to eat with him or her tomorrow. Follow through with a phone call to confirm.

- Whether you are a guest or an employee, abide by the rules of the cafeteria. Pick up after yourself.

- If you have a complaint about the cafeteria, take it to the person designated to receive them. Don't complain while going through the line or at the table.

THE EXECUTIVE DINING ROOM

Lunching in an executive dining room or boardroom follows the same format as the business lunch except the selection may be limited and there is no bill presented at the end of the meal. The food is usually simple but excellent with the surroundings quiet and elegant.

- It is not necessary to have the food served. The food may be presented buffet style or at pre-set places.

- If the entree is pre-set, give your guest a choice when issuing your invitation.

- Have beverages and dessert easily accessible.

- The host is responsible for greeting guests, seeing that coats are cared for, and indicating where washrooms are located.

- Seating arrangements are important in the executive dining room. Protocol should be observed in every case where foreign and visiting business people or officials come to lunch. The most important guest sits on the host's right, the second most important guest on the host's left. The second most important host should sit opposite the host, the third and fourth most important guests would sit on his or her right and left.

- The host introduces any agenda and is responsible for keeping the talk on topic.

- The host indicates when the lunch is concluded and sees the guests out.

- The guests should respond with a typewritten thank you.

THE BOSS INVITES YOU HOME	• You and your spouse or companion are being observed. Dress with taste and good grooming.

THE BOSS
INVITES YOU
HOME

- You and your spouse or companion are being observed. Dress with taste and good grooming.

- Social manners are expected as well as excellent table manners.

- Ask how formal it is if it is not indicated in the invitation.

- Arrive on time. Ten minutes late but no later is acceptable. Never arrive early.

- Bring a gift. Flowers, top-quality chocolates, or liqueur, but not wine or liquor.

- Don't use first names unless invited to do otherwise or if you are already on a first name basis.

- Stick to social conversation unless the boss brings up business.

- Make an effort to speak to everyone.

- Personal problems should not be discussed. Don't argue with your companion.

- Don't drink too much, don't smoke unless the host indicates it is all right, and don't tell questionable jokes.

- Don't ask for seconds, but take more if it is offered and you want it.

- Eschew TV.

- Don't be the last to leave.

- Compliment the host on the evening at least once but don't gush.

- Send a handwritten thank you.

- Don't brag or name drop back at the office.

OFFICE ENTERTAINING AT HOME

Never feel that you *must* entertain people from your office unless you want to. Your career is not dependent on it. If you do entertain, send business invitations on good paper stock with the following information clearly included:

(a) Who is giving the party

(b) What kind of party it is

(c) The date, time, and place

(d) What the occasion is

(e) How to R.S.V.P.

(f) Whether spouses and guests are invited

(g) If there are any special dress requirements

(h) Map and parking directions if necessary

1. **Preparing your home**
   - Put away anything that would represent a sentimental or financial loss.
   - If you want certain rooms off-limits, close the doors.
   - Leave one bedroom open in case someone feels faint or if that is where the coats are kept.
   - Bear in mind that people use the bathroom often during a party.
   - It can be helpful to invite close friends to mix with business associates. The best time to mix friends and business is when the business people are not all from your own company.
   - Keep pets confined.
   - Arrange for children to be cared for away from the party if possible.
   - Treat hired bartenders and servers with consideration.

- Do not force dessert onto anyone. They may be diabetic, hypoglycemic or dieting.

- Do not force alcohol on anyone.

- Do not let anyone leave your party who has had too much to drink. Your guests are your responsibility.

- You can set a time limit on the party. Ask if anyone needs a lift in the direction of the first to leave. You can offer to call a cab, or walk them to their car, or get their coats. It's all a matter of vocal tone and style.

2. **Special considerations**   Keep in mind dietary and religious preferences before entertaining a large group of people in your home.

- Orthodox Jews who keep kosher don't eat shellfish or pork.

- Mormons don't drink alcohol or caffeine beverages, including soft drinks.

- Roman Catholics do not eat meat on Ash Wednesday and Good Friday. Some will not eat meat on Fridays.

- Moslems do not eat pork or shellfish or drink alcohol.

3. **If you are a guest**
- Guests should not examine anything without asking permission.

- Guests should not watch TV.

- Drink in moderation. No drugs.

- Some homes are "smoke free." At others there may be a designated room, the porch, or balcony. Abide by the rules.

- Don't indulge in romantic hijinks.

- The host, not the guest, tips any hired help.

- Send a handwritten thank you.

THE OFFICE PARTY

- Attend cheerfully. You don't have to stay for the entire time. Top executives always leave before the party reaches a crescendo.

- Be on your best behavior. Attention-getting antics and indiscretions don't make points with anyone.

- Show respect for everyone.

- Limit your drinking. No drugs.

- Don't discuss business and don't air office grievances.

- Smoke only if indicated it's allowed.

- Don't tell questionable jokes.

- If you are called upon to speak, keep it short, light, and in good taste.

- Send a typewritten note of thanks to the organizing committee.

A FINAL WORD ON WASHROOMS AND BUSINESS ETIQUETTE

At a business breakfast, lunch, or meeting, it is not necessary to rise when someone leaves or returns. A business dinner, which includes spouses, means using social manners.

- Women should not leave for the washroom in a covey.

- Don't gossip while in the washroom. Don't make any personal comments (e.g., Gee, John, I didn't know you wore a toupee).

- Don't carry on a business discussion over the basins.

- Never comment on observations made while in the washroom (e.g., the fact that Mary's hem is held up by tape is not a business item).

9

GIVING AND RECEIVING —
THE ETIQUETTE OF BUSINESS GIFTS

During affluent times, business gift giving got out of hand. The recession of the 1980s gave pause to the practice. Offices should have a policy concerning gift giving. Collecting money for everyone's birthday, baby, or retirement can be annoying and costly. If your company does have a policy, remember to inform new staff when hiring and remind your existing staff in an annual memo.

GIVING

1. **Basic considerations**

   - Never send a gift to someone which could be considered a bribe, a payoff, or an attempt to influence.

   - When sending flowers, send cut flowers to a person's home and arrangements to the office.

   - If asked to a person's home, particularly abroad, send flowers. Send them either the morning of the dinner party or the day after the party, together with an appropriate card.

   - Gifts should not be personal. Address books, travel clocks, or a good pen are "business personal" and appropriate. Clothing is not.

   - Liquor is not always the best gift. Research the recipient's taste and religious background. Scotch is a well-received gift in Japan, but a Mormon

91

or abstainer would not be pleased with the gift.

- Gifts should be beautifully wrapped. The presentation is as important as the present.

- You may use your business card as an enclosure card. Write a thoughtful note on it and put it in an envelope.

- If possible, deliver gifts personally.

- If your office collects money for various presents, it is not bad manners to say no politely and without editorializing.

- Bonuses are the best gifts employees can receive.

2. **Giving gifts to clients**

- It is appropriate to advise clients that your company has made a contribution to a charitable organization in lieu of sending corporate Christmas gifts.

- Keep gifts in good taste; they should be very carefully chosen.

- Corporate gifts should be considered gifts of goodwill.

- The gift should relate in some way to the donor's product, service, or the area the company is involved in.

- The company's logo should be on the gift, inconspicuously, or on the handwritten card enclosed.

3. **Giving gifts to secretaries**

- It is not necessary to recognize birthdays.

- Under no circumstances give a gift of clothing.

- Reward good work with chocolates, concert tickets, or put it in writing.

- Observe National Secretary's Week (the last full week in April). Take your secretary to lunch, buy flowers or, if within your authority, give him or her the day off. Better still, do these things throughout the year.

- Your choice of Christmas gift depends on your status within the company and how long your secretary has worked for you.

- If a secretary works for more than one boss, you may get together on a gift.

4. **Giving gifts to other staff**

- If your staff has done a good job on a particular project, a gift gesture of lunch or chocolates is appropriate. (More important, acknowledge their effort in a written report to senior management.)

- At Christmas, acknowledge staff who work with you on an ongoing basis. The gift should be small, universal in appeal, and accompanied by a personal note.

- You may send a card or note to a staff member who is being married. You do not send a gift unless invited to the wedding.

- Send a card at a time of sympathy.

- Verbally acknowledge birthdays. Cards, gifts, and cakes are social manners and do not belong in a business unless it is a small, family-style organization.

- Acknowledge it in writing when a staff member has done a good job.

5. **Giving gifts to your boss**
   - The first rule is DON'T — especially if it has any overtones of "apple polishing." No staff member should feel obligated to give the boss a gift.
   - If the staff wishes to get together and give the boss a gift, that can be considered.
   - A secretary may give a gift to a boss, but should keep it modest and businesslike.

6. **Giving gifts internation-ally**

   In chapter 6, I indicated countries where gifts are expected, others where they would not be welcome. Here are some definite DON'TS when it comes to international business gifts.
   - Don't give a gift of knives to an Argentinean. (Any sharp, pointed gift to anyone should have a cork affixed to the point or be otherwise wrapped.)
   - No cowhide gifts for India. In India, the cow is sacred.
   - Don't give a striped tie to a man from Britain; he has his own school tie!
   - The law prohibits the Chinese from accepting personal gifts. The gift must be to the organization as a whole. (Don't give a clock which symbolizes death.)
   - Don't give yellow and white flowers in Germany, as those colors are associated with death.
   - In Hong Kong, present small gifts using both hands when first meeting business people.

- Don't be the first to give a business gift in Japan. Reciprocate with a slightly less expensive gift. And don't give anything in fours (e.g., four wine glasses) as Japanese associate the number four with death.

7. **The cost of the gift**

Business gifts should be kept within the range of $10 to $100 depending on the occasion and the recipient. It is only for very special clients and employees that the price of the gift should exceed $100. Executive secretaries who have worked for a long time for one boss may fall into this category.

RECEIVING

- Always acknowledge a gift with a handwritten note.

- Always accept a gift with good manners even if you already have three of the same or if it is a moose head whose nose glows in the dark. Smile and be gracious.

- If you are the head of a department and receive a gift from a client or supplier, if possible, share the gift with your staff.

- It is appropriate to return a gift when it is too expensive or too personal, when it is obscene or sexual, or when it is inappropriate (e.g., a car accessory for someone who doesn't drive).

- If you cannot accept a gift, return it at once with a short note: "I find it inappropriate to accept your gift and am returning it to you." Keep a copy of the note. Do not discuss the matter any further with the sender.

10

PUT IT IN WRITING

Throughout this book, I have indicated when thank-you notes, typewritten or handwritten, should be sent. Whenever you have to send congratulations, condolences, or thanks, choose your words carefully and be sure of your presentation. Always check your spelling and grammar and be sure names are spelled correctly. I know of a business deal that died because a thank you note was sent to Jeff instead of Geoff.

Here are some basic considerations concerning good etiquette in writing.

- Written thanks are more correct and special than telephoned thanks.

- Thank you notes should not be acknowledged.

- Gifts should always be acknowledged with a handwritten thank-you note.

- Send notes of congratulations on a marriage to those with whom you regularly do business.

- Notes and cards should not be sent on birthdays. Spoken greetings are sufficient.

- Condolences should be handwritten.

- Send handwritten notes of congratulations to the newly promoted.

- All lunch and dinner invitations should be acknowledged in writing after the event.

- Write your notes on quality 5" x 7" notepaper with your company name and your name in small embossed letters. Cream, taupe, or gray paper may be used, but nothing bright and flashy unless you are in the entertainment or fashion business.

- You may also write notes on "informals" which are folded notes 4¾" x 3½" or larger. Just your name appears engraved on the front. Alternatively, you can use correspondence cards that are 6½" x 4½", which have your name engraved at the top.

- All business stationery should show respect for the company, the employees, and the recipients. Business stationery and what is written on it reflects the image of the company.

- All business letters and notes should be signed by hand. Letters with stamped signatures indicate mass production or lack of interest in the recipient.

- Never write anything when angry. Sleep on it, or write it down, tear it up, and then sleep on it.

- Business stationery should not used for personal correspondence.

- Do not write business letters or notes on hotel stationery. Take stationery with you or wait until you are back in the office.

TITLES AND NAMES

- In business, you can use just the first and last name with no title (e.g., Joe Smith). When writing more traditional companies, use the more formal form:

  (a) Unmarried women — Miss (But see note on use of Ms. below.)

  (b) Married women — Mrs. used with the Christian name and last name (e.g., Mrs. Jane Smith —*not* Mrs. Jack Smith).

  (c) Widows — Mrs. used with Christian name and last name.

  (d) Men — Mr.

  (e) In business correspondence, when you use a professional title, use it after the surname (e.g., Joe Smith, M.D.; Jill Black, Ph.D.)

- Because the way we address people is in a state of change, if you can, it is wise to telephone the office of the person you are writing to and ask how that person prefers to be addressed. Some women may insist on Ms.; others may prefer tradition.

- If a business woman marries and uses her husband's name or combines both names, she should send announcements to that effect to those with whom she regularly does business.

BUSINESS CARDS

- Business cards should be clean, up to date, and of good quality.

- Do not force your card on anyone or offer it early in conversation.

- Do not fling your cards about like flyers at a supermarket opening.

- Do not give out business cards at a social gathering, but do have some with you in case someone asks for one. Then be discreet in presenting it.

- Use your business card when sending flowers or a gift. Personalize it with a note on the back.

- Use your business card when forwarding material or a resume to someone. Once again, personalize it with a note.

- Present your business card to the receptionist when visiting a company for the first time. It helps the receptionist announce you.

- Present your business card when calling a new client.

- Ask for a business card when you are sincere about wanting to remember the person and the company, for whatever reason.

- Receive business cards graciously. You may place them in the back of your card case. Be sure to remove and file them periodically or you may find yourself giving out someone else's card.

BUSINESS ANNOUNCEMENT CARDS

It is extremely good business etiquette to send business news by way of an announcement card. A card gets the recipient's attention and can effectively announce a change of address, new phone number, new appointments, or promotion.

- Use good quality stock with the message either printed or engraved.

- You may add a personal note if you wish.

- Envelopes should be typewritten, handwritten, or printed on a word processor. Never use labels.

- Business announcements need not be acknowledged by the recipient, but it is good etiquette to send a note of congratulations to anyone who has been promoted.

11

MANNERS ON THE ROAD

When you travel on business, the operative word is business. Use your time well, whether in the air or on the ground. Do not indulge in any sexual peccadillos or wild adventures. Business trips are not the time to "taste life." When traveling on business, by yourself or with associates, abide by good business etiquette and decorum.

SOME BASIC CONSIDERATIONS

- Keep luggage light and compact. Don't expect anyone else to carry it for you.

- Carry a travel alarm. Don't rely on anyone else to wake you.

- If you are going abroad, be sure to take voltage adapters. It is very poor manners to start a fire in a hotel!

- Invest in a compact, easy-to-use travel steamer. Rumpled clothing is offensive.

- Coordinate your wardrobe to get the most out of a few pieces.

- Be on time for departures.

- Remember your hellos, pleases, and thank yous to air travel staff. (No tipping.)

- Abide by the rules, no smoking signs, and seat belt regulations.

- Keep your alcohol intake to a minimum at all times. No drugs.

- It is not bad manners to *not* talk to a seat companion if you don't know him or her. Immerse yourself in work, a book, or put on the headset. You don't have to turn it on.

- Plan to arrive a day ahead for an important long distance meeting to avoid jet lag.

- Keep daily notes on names, progress, and procedures so you can use them on your next visit.

- If you use someone's office or facilities during a business trip, bring a suitable gift (e.g., chocolates) to give on your departure.

- Your evenings may be your own, but you are still your company's representative. Don't take chances. Don't do anything that would embarrass you or your company.

- Don't share rooms. You need to rest and be yourself. Pay the difference for privacy.

- Don't let your room become the "after business" party room.

- If you don't want to eat alone in the dining room, order room service.

- If you don't want company in a bar, take work with you. Better still, use the valet bar in your room.

- Conduct business on your client's premises or rent a suite to do so. Never conduct business in your room.

- Eat lightly and get enough sleep.

TIPPING AND TRAVEL	• Taxi drivers should be tipped 10% to 15% of the fare.
	• Bellhops are usually given $1 per bag; chambermaids get $1 to $2 per day.
	• Consider your order when you use room service. If you just ordered a sandwich, 15% may not be enough.
	• For shoe shine service, put your tip in an envelope when you place your shoes out to be shined.
TRAVELING TOGETHER	• One person can be in charge of paying for all expenses. If you dine separately, put the charge on your room bill.
	• The junior defers to the senior. That means sitting on the jump seat in the limousine or the middle seat in the back of the car.
	• Don't engage in long, personal conversations. You are still on business.
	• When traveling in a corporate jet, be early, take the seat designated, treat the crew with respect, and eat what is offered.
	• There is no need to spend all your free time with your fellow travelers. You may wish to have dinner on your own. Let them know in advance.

STAYING AT SOMEONE'S HOME

On a business trip, it is best not to stay at the home of your client or associate. If you do, or if you stay with friends, keep these tips in mind:

- Spend some time with your hosts, but do not infringe on their routine.

- Abide by the house rules.

- Take your hosts out to dinner.

- Give a gift before leaving.

MEETING VISITING TRAVELERS

- You don't have to be a tour guide and are not expected to entertain them each evening. Use common sense.

- Be on time if meeting a plane or train.

- Help with the luggage, and get your guests settled at their hotel.

- Have an office and phone set aside for their use.

- Have your secretary assist them wherever necessary.

- When you are out together, pick up the bill.

THE CONFERENCE OR CONVENTION

- Your company is not paying for your pleasure. Attend sessions, make notes, and get your business dollars worth.

- Don't ruin your reputation by over-staying your welcome at hospitality suites.

- Be on time for sessions.

- Introduce yourself to others. Have a lot of business cards on hand.

- Keep a positive attitude.

- Let people know when they've made a good speech or conducted an excellent session.

104

- If your spouse or companion is attending a conference social event with you, make sure introductions are made. Be sure your spouse or companion is made to feel part of the group.

- Don't wear your name tag outside of the conference area. (It's very classy to have a name tag made that you can carry in your briefcase and use when tags are necessary. Then you can avoid glue on your best suit or pinholes in your silk blouse.)

- If you make promises to send materials to someone, do so as soon as you get back to the office. (Keep notes all through the conference.)

- Sending a letter of congratulations for a well-run conference or convention is good etiquette.

12
DRESS AND DECORUM

So much has been written about what to wear and what not to wear for business; this chapter reviews the basics. First, it is important to wear clothing that is appropriate, of good quality, and in good taste. More important is being clean, well groomed, and cared for. Most important is your attitude toward yourself, your work, and others.

I have seen business people dressed in the latest styles, the right colors, wearing only "real" jewelry, carrying beautiful briefcases, and writing with gold fountain pens, yet wondering why they are not successful in business. But their shoulders are frosted with dandruff, they have "ring-around-the-collar," use profanity, or have a "why not me?" attitude.

It isn't what you wear that counts so much, it's how you wear it and with what style.

DO'S AND DON'TS FOR BUSINESS WARDROBES

- Do ask for help from a consultant in a reputable store, a freelance fashion consultant, or from someone whose clothes and style are indicative of good business dressing.

- Don't slavishly follow the latest fashion trends.

- Do emulate upper management in tone of dress.

- If your company has a dress code, stick to it.

SHOPPING FOR CLOTHING

- Consider the investment, for that is what clothing is. Is it good quality? Can it be in your wardrobe for more than one season? Is it a fad that calls attention to itself for one season and will be out of style the next? Don't buy heavy duty polyester that will outlast our civilization.

- Consider your type of work and the style of the company you work for.

- Consider the fit. It may be good fabric and style, but the fit is most important.

- Consider style and color. Is it right for your shape and size, your skin tone and hair? (For example, when I wear camel or black, people are very uneasy. They think I may expire before the meeting concludes.)

- Buy quality rather than quantity. Less can definitely mean more in business dressing.

- Leave sexiness out of it. Don't play to the bust, behind, or leg voyeurs.

GOOD GROOMING AND GOOD HEALTH

- Clean teeth after eating. If you have to clean your teeth in an office washroom, wash the bowl after and wipe it dry with a paper towels.

- Bathe or shower daily.

- Use deodorant, mouthwash, and a foot deodorant.

- Keep your hair well cut, washed, and well groomed. Dated haircuts and styles, grease, and excessive hair spray are not good business etiquette.

- Keep nails manicured and clean.

- Keep clothes laundered, pressed and dry cleaned. Check for stains after

107

each wearing. Sew on loose buttons. Use a lint brush.

- Keep shoes polished and in good repair; don't let heels run down.

- Use only good quality, subtle perfume, cologne, and after-shave. Remember that when you wear a scent you get used to it and cannot smell its intensity any longer.

- If you wear jogging shoes to work, change both socks and shoes when you arrive. Socks and hose absorb the perspiration of walking and can be offensive for the rest of the day.

- Replace frayed watch bands.

- Keep your briefcase well polished and in good repair. Replace it when necessary. Do not put decals on your briefcase. Regularly clean out the lint and bits of paper.

- Maintain a good relationship with your doctor and dentist. Stained, decaying, or missing teeth can be very offensive.

- Stay home when you are ill. It is poor manners to share germs or to expect sympathy for any illness.

- Descriptions of operations or medical procedures do not belong in the office.

- If you have a health condition that requires medication or monitoring such as a heart condition, diabetes, or epilepsy, the people you work with should be aware of it and know what to do in case of emergency.

Always wear a Medical Alert brace-
let.

FOR BUSINESS
WOMEN

- Dress with decorum. That means no
  mini skirts, even though fashion ma-
  vens may be pushing them as the
  latest thing, no low-cut blouses or
  bursting buttons, no tight clothing,
  and no flashy jewelry.

- Keep nails fairly short. In some countries long nails are worn to indicate
  the wearer doesn't work. False nails
  are associated with performers in entertainment rather than business. No
  gold or speckled nails. Undercloth-
  ing should not be visible and always
  fresh and clean.

- Wear makeup that is fresh and mod-
  erate. No false eyelashes, please.

- Keep an emergency kit that includes
  sewing necessities, toothbrush and
  toothpaste, extra pantyhose (neutral
  shade), nail polish and emery board,
  lint brush, comb and mirror, hair
  spray, deodorant, tampons, and
  shoe buffer.

- Keep skirts pressed — no wrinkles or
  bulges.

- Never wear clothing made of fabrics
  like velvet, satin, brocade, or sequins
  — more appropriate for evening
  wear — to the office.

- Never wear "western" fabrics to the
  office (i.e., jean materials, bandana
  fabrics) unless you're in Calgary at
  stampede time.

- Never wear white shoes or carry a
  white purse. If you wish to wear

them, do so only between May 24 and Labor Day. (Never wear them in England; there, white shoes are worn only in the country.)

- Think twice about changing the color of your hair or wearing wigs of different styles and colors. It's confusing for associates and can label you as indecisive or flamboyant.

- Always blot lipstick after application. Leaving a red impression on glasses and cups is very poor etiquette.

- Wear jewelry in moderation — no jangling, clanging bracelets.

- Wear well-made quality shoes with a low or medium heel. Avoid ankle straps, sandals, and "fussy" shoes for business.

- Never wear lacy stockings or fancy pantyhose to work.

- Make constant wardrobe checks for frayed blouses, shiny skirts, or cracked and worn leather. Replace items when necessary.

- Never put your handbag on a desk, boardroom table, or restaurant table. (Consider investing in a briefcase that incorporates a purse within its design.)

- Never wear a pantsuit to the office. The exception is if your work takes you out into the field.

FOR BUSINESS MEN

- Dress with decorum. Leave the wild and wonderful to Las Vegas. Avoid overly tight pants, flashy jewelry, and watches that tell everything including the tides.

- Some companies want no facial hair whatever. Keep mustaches and beards clean and trimmed.

- Hair in the ears and nostrils is offensive.

- Underwear should be fresh and clean.

- Keep an emergency kit that includes toothbrush and toothpaste, comb, lint brush, nail file and clippers, a fresh shirt and a tie (a soup-stained tie does not impress), razor, deodorant, and shoe buffer.

- Use handkerchiefs, not small tissues.

- Wear executive-length socks so that no hairy shank is exposed when you cross your legs.

13

SEXUAL HARASSMENT IN YOUR WORKPLACE

THE PROBLEM

One of the most serious behavioral issues facing business today is sexual harassment in the workplace. This is far more serious than any of the other business etiquette subjects addressed in this book for it can result in lawsuits, sullied reputations, and ruined careers.

What was discussed in previous chapters has to do with freely chosen attitudes and behavior. It's up to you whether you want to slouch, slurp, snore, or ignore. You make the decision dependent on how serious you are about your career advancement. However, sexual harassment is quite another issue. It is not something to be facetious about for it is not about choices. It is about law. It affects everyone from owner to manager, supervisor to employee.

The issue became widely publicized as a result of the televised hearings in the Thomas-Hill U.S. Senate investigation in 1991, but as early as the 1970s national surveys in the United States showed that 40% to 60% of women questioned reported being harassed at work. With more and more women entering the work force and, in particular, traditional male jobs, the problem has become apparent in big and small businesses. "Women Employed," a national membership of women at all levels of employment, estimated in 1991 that 45% of the 58 million women employed in the United States experience harassment in the lifetime of their careers.

Companies, big and small, have found that sexual harassment is a major problem that cannot be ignored. The December, 1988 issue of *Working Women* carried the results of its survey among women working for Fortune 500 companies.

The statistics were shocking: 90% of the companies had received complaints of sexual harassment; more than one-third had been hit with lawsuits and 64% of their personnel officers said most complaints were valid. Two-thirds of the complaints were against immediate supervisors and upper management. A typical Fortune 500 company ended up paying an average of $282.53 per employee per year: $6.7 million in absenteeism, employee turnover, and low productivity.

Sexual harassment at work is not just a North American problem: 70% of Japanese women and 50% of European women surveyed reported being sexually harassed. Nor are all victims women; 15% percent of men surveyed had been harassed by co-workers of both sexes. Often too, sexual harassment follows an inner-company romance that has gone sour. The U.S. Society for Human Resource Management reports that 1 out of 20 sexual harassment cases cannot be filed because the situation of harassment was originally consensual.

WHAT IS SEXUAL HARASSMENT?

Sexual harassment is not about sex. It is about power. Studies show that most sexual harassment is from a superior to a subordinate. Studies also show that the higher the relative number of men, the higher the harassment. When women workers equal male workers or are the majority, they are treated as fellow workers, when in the minority they are treated as a minority group with lower status. Very often men and women perceive sexual harassment differently. For example, studies show that men are flattered by sexual comments by women, while women are more often repulsed. An individual's upbringing, attitudes and beliefs can also cause differences in perception of what is or is not sexual harassment.

TWO TYPES OF SEXUAL HARASSMENT

There are two main types of sexual harassment: quid pro quid (you give me this, I'll give you that) and hostile work environment. Quid pro quid is all about power. It is sexual blackmail. The work environment is all about war and pollution; verbal and physical pollution of a worker's personal environment which leads to hostility.

The U.S. Equal Employment Opportunity Commission (EEOC) passed federal guidelines in 1980 defining sexual harassment as unwelcome sexual advances, requests for sexual favors, and other verbal or physical conduct of a sexual nature when submission to such conduct is made either explicitly or implicitly a term or condition of an individual's employment or when submission to or rejection of such conduct by an individual is used as the basis for employment decisions affecting such individuals (e.g., promotions, raises).

Such conduct has the purpose or effect of unreasonably interfering with an individual's work performance or creating an intimidating, hostile, or offensive working environment (unwanted behavior which is sexual in nature).

WHO IS SEXUALLY HARASSED?

Ninety percent of workers who experience harassment are women between the ages of 24 and 34. (Men who experience harassment are slightly older.) Most women who are sexually harassed are divorced, separated, or single. They are most likely to be in a low wage bracket and not as well educated as the harasser.

WHO ARE THE HARASSERS?

Harassers are usually older, married men who are not attractive to their victims. They usually hold a position of power over the harassed. In some cases, they are simply insensitive to the situation and unaware that their humor, comments, or actions are not appreciated. Others are hard core harassers using their positions to intimidate, manipulate, and blackmail.

Men can be harassed by homosexual men or by women. In either case the harasser usually holds a position of power over the harassed.

WHAT ABOUT YOU?

Let's get down to some specifics to help you. As I have emphasized, sexual harassment goes far beyond acceptable business manners. You may be excused for boorish business behavior, but you will not be excused, nor should you excuse someone else for sexual harassment in your place of work. First look at your own behavior. Ask yourself if you:

- Tell inappropriate jokes.

- Make sexual comments to members of the opposite sex with whom you work.

- Compliment co-workers on their looks, rather than on how they accomplish their work.

- Hug, pinch, or pat.

- Make "good-natured" comments: "How's your love life?," "How's that good-looking wife of yours?"

If you answer yes to any of these you had better clean up your act and start to adopt some very positive action. Here are some guidelines for personal behavior:

- Assess your self-image at work. Does it project how you wish to be treated?

- Adhere to the sexual harassment policy of your company at all times.

- Be businesslike in conduct and action. Follow the advice given in previous chapters of this book.

- Show respect for yourself, your fellow workers, and anyone connected with work.

- Dress in a professional, appropriate manner. While this cannot be an issue in sexual harassment cases, it can send a clear signal about how you feel about your work. (In some court cases sexually provocative speech and dress have been relative in determining if an employee found sexual overtures welcome.) However, unless there is an employee-approved dress code, personnel cannot be pressured to change their mode of dress. Just use common sense and set a standard for yourself.

HOW DO YOU KNOW IF YOU ARE BEING SEXUALLY HARASSED?

Your own behavior might be exemplary toward your fellow employees, but that does not say that others act as you do. Some harassment is blatant, some is subtle. What one person can consider good-natured horseplay another might find very offensive. If you feel you are being illegally sexually harassed ask yourself these questions before you act:

- Did the harassment occur because of my sex?

- Is it related to or about sex?

- Is the behavior toward me unwelcome, not returned and not mutual? (It is important to keep in mind that if you previously accepted, condoned, or participated in the behavior, it will be hard to prove it is now unwelcome.)

- Is the behavior directed to other employees of the same gender?

- Has the person behaved this way toward others in the past?

- Despite my asking for the behavior to stop, has it continued?

- Is the behavior toward me interfering with my work?

- Is there an implication that I must accept the behavior or respond to it if I wish to keep my job or advance my position?

- Is the behavior creating a hostile or intimidating or offensive environment in which I must work?

- Do I feel demeaned, threatened, embarrassed, or degraded by the behavior toward me?

If you have answered yes to the above questions, you may well be in a situation of sexual harassment. Remember, the more severe the behavior is, the fewer times it must be repeated to be sexual harassment. The less severe, the more it must be repeated.

WHAT TO DO WHEN SEXUALLY HARASSED

When you have determined that you are being sexually harassed, do not deny or excuse the harasser. Denial only keeps you from dealing with the problem and allows the harasser to continue.

- Do not blame yourself. If you have done nothing to provoke unwanted sexual harassment then you are not to blame.

- Do not ignore the harasser. Seventy-five percent of the time the situation only gets worse if you try to ignore it.

- Do not try to cope by avoiding the harasser. This can only affect your job performance.

- Do take action.

- Appraise the situation calmly.

- Keep a level head.

- Be firm. Don't be overly dramatic or angry.

117

- Let your body language support your words.

- Tell the offender, calmly and directly, that the behavior is offensive to you and should not be repeated. For example: "When you call me baby and put your arm around me I feel very offended because I want to be treated as an adult and have your respect."

You are not being hostile or confrontational. By using the "I" approach you are not placing blame.

Or you can make a specific request: "Please don't tell me those jokes. I don't find them funny and they make me feel embarrassed."

- Document the incident.

- Document your meeting.

- Tell someone else about the situation, particularly your supervisor. Document the meeting.

- If the offense is repeated, follow procedures for filing a complaint.

- Don't deal with severe situations yourself. Get help immediately.

A FINAL WORD

I advise you to know the company you work for well before filing a complaint. Determine the following:

- Were previous complaints from other employees handled quickly? If not, demand action on your complaint.

- Were complaints taken seriously? If not, then make sure that you have documentation and witnesses.

- Was correct time given to complaints or were they rushed or dragged on? Be sure you ask appropriate interview time with the appropriate people.

- Were past investigations fair to all parties? If not, insist on a review.

- Did past investigations result in action? Was the harassment stopped? Was the harasser disciplined appropriately? Was the victim provided support and options? If not, keep in mind from the outset that you may have to refile your complaint.

Choose a company to work for that assures you a sexually harassment-free environment — a company that will stand behind you if you are harassed by clients, suppliers, or anyone else connected with doing company business. If the company you work for does not have a sexual harassment policy impress upon management the importance of one. (The Appendix at the back of this book provides guidelines for creating a sexual harassment policy in any business.)

Men and women who work independently have to set the tone for their own work environment. Good common sense can prevail.

- Don't conduct business in a hotel room.

- Keep your business hours within the 8:00 a.m. to 5:00 p.m. spectrum, dress appropriately, use no alcoholic beverages or other stimulants, keep idle chit chat to a minimum and not on personal subjects, and refrain from personal contact beyond a business-like handshake.

- Should it be necessary, inform the other person of your own personal policy regarding dating, sexual jokes, and comments. Be firm but not hostile.

- Remember, conduct yourself as a professional business person. Don't allow yourself to be either a victim or a harasser.

14

EPILOGUE — SOCIAL MANNERS

I said at the outset that business etiquette is based on the premise that men and women should be treated equally, as colleagues. I have also stated several times, especially when referring to business abroad, when social manners toward women are expected. From my observation of business people, I find that most of those over 45 have these social skills, but many under 45 do not. So, here are some basic social skills that will serve you in good stead when you are out socially, both at home and abroad.

Social manners are expected when you are out for dinner with associates, their spouses, or companions, and when you attend a concert, play, or opera.

ESPECIALLY FOR MEN

A gentleman —

- Opens doors for a lady.

- Hangs up her coat.

- Holds her chair and helps to seat her. (However, in some restaurants the maitre d' does the seating, at which time the gentleman stands until she is seated.)

- Stands when a lady enters the room, and remains standing until she is seated. Stands when a lady stands.

- When dining, orders for her, after ascertaining her preference, and always pays.

- Serves the lady first, before himself.

121

- Carries packages for her.

- Has her precede him, following the usher or maitre d' or into the taxi.

- Walks on the curb side to keep her from being splashed or on the building side to keep her from being mugged (locale dictates protocol).

- Always assists her into her coat.

- Picks up anything she drops.

- Steps back to allow her to exit from an elevator.

- Always removes his hat in an elevator if a lady is present.

A smart business man will recognize that social manners are an asset. He will be well versed in both business and social manners and be able to use whichever the occasion demands.

ESPECIALLY FOR WOMEN

A lady —

- Allows a gentleman to be a gentleman and do the things as described above, with gracious thanks.

A smart business woman —

- Recognizes that many business visitors to North America will use social manners even during business hours.

- Never chastises a man for using social manners.

- Recognizes that older executives have had to go through a culture shock and may, out of habit, still use social manners in a business situation.

- Uses "gentlemen's social manners" herself when with an elderly woman in a social situation where no men are present, particularly when abroad.

THE FINAL WORD

Finally, here is a review of the good manners your parents should have taught you that have nothing to do with gender or society, but everything to do with recognition and promotion.

- Always be punctual. If you are going to be late, let people know.

- Don't be afraid to apologize.

- Always give credit when credit is due.

- Keep your promises.

- Be thoughtful to another's feelings, space, and property.

- Do not use the witty quip that degrades another.

- Don't boast.

- Don't name drop.

- Don't talk about how much something costs — to do so is very gauche.

- Never gossip or repeat a rumor.

- Go out of your way to put others at ease.

- Call immediately if you're unable to attend a social function to which you've accepted an invitation.

- Never bring a guest to a social function unless asked to do so.

- Pick up the bar bill when it's your turn. Always have cash or a credit card with you. A "sponger" is no reputation to have in business.

- Pay for the coffee if there's a container to do so. Wash your cup. Make fresh coffee.

- Never push, literally or figuratively.

- No matter what rung of the ladder you are on, use real things: real cups, not plastic; really good hangers, not wire; a good print instead of a poster.

- Don't make your office into a jungle of unattended plants. Keep one healthy plant or bring yourself cut flowers each week. Uncared for, dying plants and flowers are offensive to many.

- Say please, thank you, and you're welcome.

- Fill the paper tray in the copy room.

- Never drink directly from a soda pop can unless outdoors where no glass is available.

- Cover your mouth when you sneeze or yawn.

- Always have a handkerchief with you.

- Never shout, but speak to be heard and understood.

- Cultivate a well-modulated voice.

- Use good grammar; put the final sounds on words.

These points reiterate some that I have already made in this book, but it is upon these small points that your business reputation is built.

I urge you to let good business etiquette become a natural part of your life so that you have a confident, respectful, and respected style that becomes as natural to you as your other business skills: a style that will travel well and be acceptable to everyone regardless of age, race, creed, sex, or sexual preference.

FORMING A SEXUAL HARASSMENT POLICY FOR YOUR BUSINESS

WHY SHOULD COMPANIES HAVE A SEXUAL HARASSMENT POLICY?

While rules of etiquette for most business situations do not have to be written down as a company policy, those concerned with sexual harassment should, for these three reasons:

- Owners and management have concern for the well-being of their employees.

- Owners and management have concern for their public image.

- If there is no policy the business, owners and management could be subject to legal intervention.

All management, of large or small companies, can learn from Prudential Life which has a long-standing policy that contains the warning that romantic relationships can influence the quality of decisions and potentially hurt other people. It goes on to consider every aspect of sexual harassment. DuPont has one of the most extensive sexual harassment prevention and education programs which includes a 24-hour hot line, seminars, and, when necessary, a team of investigators.

No matter what your position — owner, manager, supervisor, or employee — this is one area of business behavior that you cannot ignore. Owners and managers are the wellspring for setting example and policy for they are ultimately liable. Supervisors should have their fingers on the pulse of their departments. Whatever happens within that department is ultimately their responsibility. Employees should insist that the companies they work for have a sexual harassment policy. Such a policy spells out for everyone, from the top down, what behavior is acceptable and what is not.

WHO IS RESPONSIBLE FOR A COMPANY'S POLICY?

Owners and managers of the business are responsible for setting up and maintaining the proper work atmosphere and the reporting procedures. If a business supports, allows, or accepts sexual harassment, then sexual harassment will be more prevalent.

Unless there is a well-communicated and strictly enforced sexual harassment policy in place, a business can face legal action from an employee. Businesses should have a written policy stating that it opposes and prohibits harassment. Good examples of what is meant by harassment should be given. It should be signed by the owner and the manager. If there are co-owners, partners, or other executives, they should sign it also.

HOW TO FORMULATE A POLICY FOR YOUR BUSINESS

If the company you work for does not have a sexual harassment policy, one should be initiated immediately. No company should be without one. However, it is not something that should be slapped together. For that reason, I am explicit about the steps to follow. (If your company already has a policy you can use the steps to measure its effectiveness.)

Management should work with employees to formulate policy and procedures regarding sexual harassment. Employees should be part of the team, able to express their thoughts and opinions.

Step 1: Drafting a dating policy

A dating policy should particularly address the supervisor-subordinate relationship. AT&T, for example, with 7,500 married couples in the company, has a strong policy on sexual harassment which discourages direct supervisor-subordinate dating and forbids spouse reporting to spouse. Apple Computer does not allow employees any direct reporting or contractual relationship with anyone with whom they have a significant personal relationship. However, while sexual harassment is illegal, romance is not! Employees must be in agreement with a dating policy.

What should go into a dating policy? Consider the following:

- Any office liaison that causes employees to complain or gossip will not be tolerated.

- If there is a complaint or persistent prevailing rumor, the manager will discuss it with the individuals named reminding them that the alleged affair is in direct violation of company policy and if it is happening, it should stop, or other alternatives need to be considered.

- The manager will discuss those alternatives such as a transfer or buy out.

- If there has been an affair which has ended, the manager may still consider transfers to avoid future work or personality problems.

- Misuse of company time and expense money to pursue a personal relationship will not be tolerated.

You might consider a softer approach: If a relationship develops between two employees, they should approach their supervisor for a work solution before it becomes a problem. (This approach helps responsible people find a good solution that will enable them to stay with the company.)

Step 2: Defining sexual harassment offenses

Open discussion between management and employees should result in what they consider to be sexual harassment. Here are some examples:

- Compliments to do with physical looks and attributes (e.g., build, figure, hair, eyes, legs, dimples.)

- Compliments to do with clothing, particularly the fit.

- Tone of voice. "My, you look nice today" may be an innocent compliment, but if it is said in a sultry, slow tone of voice with the eyes moving up and down the body, it becomes something else. The words are innocent but the tone and accompanying action are not.

- Recounting dreams or fantasies about a person to that person or anyone else.

- Speculating about an individual's physical attributes or sexual prowess, whether to that individual or to others.

- Telling vulgar, off-color, sexually explicit, or demeaning anecdotes or jokes. (It doesn't change the situation to say, "Oops, sorry, Mary." or "Cover your ears.")

- Unwanted personal notes; repeated, unwanted invitations. (No means no!)

- Posters, pictures, coffee mugs, and T-shirts that are offensive or carry offensive messages.

- Offensive practical jokes or unwanted gifts. (Finding a jockstrap on your desk every morning is not funny; it is sexual harassment.)

- Any discussion, remarks or speculation to do with an individual's sexual preference, sexual functions, or sexual health.

Discussions should also include what physical actions constitute sexual harassment. Here are some examples:

Wolf whistles
Winking
Patting
Blocking and cornering
Brushing up against a person
Pinching
Grabbing
Back or neck rubs
Touching hair
Touching hands
"Footsies" or "kneesies"
Staring up and down

If you think these actions happen only to women, you are wrong. The first call on the first open line radio show I ever did was from a man whose female boss was committing five of these offenses against him!

Discussions should include what words and phrases constitute sexual harassment. If you walk by any schoolyard in North America, you will hear language that should burn the mouth and is obviously inappropriate in any business setting. But also include in your discussion words and phrases that some people may not consider inappropriate, but others do. Some may be a surprise to those who have been using them. Men, who for years, have been calling women "honey" or "babe" may be surprised to find it is not considered a compliment by most women. In business, men want to be called men and women, women. Be careful about euphemisms that may not be considered offensive by some, but certainly will be by others (e.g., "female problem," "time of the month," "queer"). That language has no place in your work place.

Step 3: Getting a policy down on paper

Once a business determines what it wants in its sexual harassment policy, it should see that such a policy is written in strong, clear language. It should be majority approved by

131

owners, managers, supervisors, and employees — and the company lawyer, just to be on the safe side. Here is an example of a business policy on sexual harassment:

> You are guaranteed an environment where you can work free from all forms of discrimination including sexual harassment. You are valued and promoted based on your job performance. You, our employee, male or female, will not be subjected to unsolicited and unwelcome sexual overtures or conduct, verbal or physical.

> Sexual harassment is unwelcome behavior which is offensive to another. None of the following will be tolerated: repeated, unwanted sexual flirtation; advances or propositions; repeated verbal abuse of a sexual nature; degrading or graphic comments about an individual's appearance; any offensive or abusive physical contact; the display of sexually suggestive objects, pictures or posters.

> Additionally, no one will imply or threaten that you should be "sexually cooperative" or that refusal will have any effect on your employment, career development, career advancement, compensation, assignments, or any other condition of employment.

> Managers, supervisors, non-supervisory personnel, and non-employees are covered by this policy. Conduct of sexual harassment is prohibited and disciplinary action will be taken if this policy is violated.

> Questions regarding this policy or a specific situation should be addressed to your supervisor or the head of personnel. Procedural steps are outlined in your employee manual. Confidentiality is assured.

> Remember: We have a written policy against sexual harassment. We have a procedure whereby sexual harassment can be regis-

tered. We take complaints seriously. We take
appropriate remedial action.

Having a policy in place that leads to disciplinary action
informs all employees that a company is not just giving lip
service to a very important business behavioral problem. A
policy that assures employees have a recourse for complaint
and that complaints can be filed, addressed, and resolved
without the involvement of outside authority is the corner-
stone to being perceived as a responsible, up-to-date business.

Step 4: Specific procedures for reporting sexual harassment

Accompanying any policy on sexual harassment should be a
procedure for reporting harassment. Once again, it should be
worked out with and approved by all personnel. Procedures
could also encourage employees to —

- Personally establish and clearly articulate boundaries concerning dating co-workers if there is no company dating policy.

- Clearly articulate comfort level concerning jokes and pranks.

- Know the boundaries and comfort
  level of fellow employees and respect them.

- Let the person know that he or she is
  harassing you and you want it
  stopped.

- Confide in someone else if you feel
  you are being harassed.

- Report the harassment if it continues.

Here is a sample of what a sexual harassment complaint
report should contain:

- Your name, position, address, home
  phone number.

- Name, address, and position of individual you feel sexually discriminated against you.

- Give exact date(s) and time(s) of acts of discrimination.

- If this is a repeated act or if there is more than one person involved, give all names, dates, times, and places of the harassment.

- Describe the act of sexual harassment.

- If possible, give names and positions of witnesses who are willing to support or substantiate your story.

- Describe how this conduct has affected your work.

- Describe how this conduct has affected your personal life.

- State whether you would prefer your complaint to be heard by a man or woman. (There should be a choice of reporting to male or female. Women are sometimes reluctant to discuss harassment complaints with a man.)

- If any individual intimidates, threatens, coerces, or discriminates against you for the purpose of interfering with the investigation of this complaint, document the actions and file an additional complaint.

An employee should file a complaint with his or her supervisor or with the head of personnel. (There should be a choice since most sexual harassment complaints involve superior-subordinate.) An employee should also keep a copy of the complaint report.

Employees also need guidelines for behavior if they are charged with sexual harassment. Retaliation is against the law, but in our imperfect world a disgruntled employee could use a sexual harassment charge as vindication for not getting promoted or for a poor job review. An avenue must be provided so that the person charged can respond. For example, guidelines may advise:

- If you are accused informally of sexual harassment, get the specifics. What did you do or say to prompt the accusation? If it is truly a misunderstanding, let the accuser know you did not intend to make him or her uncomfortable. Apologize, preferably in front of witnesses.

- Document the conversation in case the accusation goes further. It is important to show you had no intention of making unwanted advances or were being discriminatory in any way.

- Do not repeat the offense.

- In the future, if possible, work with or communicate with the accuser in the company of others.

- Do not be vindictive in any way.

Guidelines should also advise an employee what to do if a formal sexual complaint is filed against him or her. Here is an example of procedural guidelines:

- Be sure you understand the complaint.

- Be ready to answer specific questions.

- Bring any documentation you may have made.

- Check the dates in the complaint against your own calendar.

- If possible, have names of witnesses who can support or substantiate your story.

- If an apology is in order and would be satisfactory, sincerely give one.

- If charges are valid, accept the consequences.

- If you feel you are the victim of an unjustified accusation in retaliation for some other action, file your own grievance, supported by documentation and any witnesses.

Step 5: Procedures for investigating a complaint

Part of a sexual harassment program must be the mechanism to investigate the complaint. This is not easy. There must be concern about retaliation, vindictiveness, slander, privacy, reputation, who is telling the truth, and what is to be gained or lost.

Whoever receives and investigates the complaint must determine whether sexual harassment has happened. Here are some guidelines for investigating a sexual harassment complaint.

- Take all complaints seriously.

- Document everything.

- Get the complaint in writing following the proper procedures for complaint.

- Act immediately to meet the complainant in private.

- Be open and supportive to the complainant.

- Do not be judgmental.

- Listen carefully. Do not joke about or belittle the charge.

- Offer to meet the victim and the offender together. Do not make excuses for the offender.

- Arrange to hear the other side.

- If you are convinced that sexual harassment has occurred you must stop it immediately and discipline the offender.

- If you are convinced that no harassment has occurred, counsel both the complainant and the accused.

- Counselling for both should be part of the process no matter what the outcome.

- Be sure no retaliation occurs.

- Arrange for work separation if necessary.

- If you feel the need for your own character protection, have another person sit in on the hearing.

- Confidentiality must be assured. No one must be unfairly treated because a complaint has been made.

The procedure for hearing a complaint should be approved by all staff. It should be generated through discussion with them and be published in the employee manual. It must be adhered to without prejudice. The wording in the manual may be similar to the following:

Immediately upon receipt of your written complaint of sexual harassment a private, unbiased hearing will be scheduled. Your complaint will be taken seriously and heard without prejudgment. The accused will be given the same opportunity. If sexual harassment is determined, action will be taken.

If either you or the accused are dissatisfied with the results of the hearing, you may ask that another be set.

Step 6: Disciplinary action

A sexual harassment program must have an action component. Offenders must know their behavior will not be tolerated and if sexual harassment is proven appropriate action will be taken. Once again, decisions for action should be reached through employee discussion and approval, but it is ultimately the employer's responsibility to deal with the harasser. Once approved it is policy and should be included in the employee manual or handbook.

Here are some guidelines for action:

- Inform the offender that the complaint violates company policy and action will be taken.

- Action may include education, transfer, demotion, or discharge. Discharge certainly follows if the offender is repeating behavior that he or she has been previously warned about or charged with.

- The offender's overall record and the seriousness of the misconduct must be considered.

- Decide on the corrective action. Is a verbal reprimand and warning enough? Would the complainant be satisfied with giving the offender a warning and receiving an apology? Does the charge call for much more serious action?

- Advise the offender of the corrective action.

- Follow up to make sure the action is taken.

- Consider if compensation is due the complainant: was there loss of job title, pay, conditions of employment?

Businesses cannot afford to keep hard-core harassers. These angry, hostile people continually embarrass and intimidate co-workers. When confronted they reply, "You just can't take a joke." or "She asked for it." or "Can't you take a compliment?" They are completely insensitive and unwilling to change. When policy statements and discipline fail to change or stop their behavior, they should not be excused, their employment should be terminated.

Step 7: Training employees

An awareness training program for old and new employees is essential in introducing and maintaining a sexual harassment education program. Personnel must understand what sexual harassment is, what company policy entails and how to resolve conflict situations. Training may be divided into two sessions: one for executives, supervisors, and managers and one for general employees. Training should start at the top and end with employees. Men and women should not be separated. Through strong implementation of the policy and awareness training, all staff will soon realize that sexual harassment will not be tolerated. It is *beneficial* to the whole process if there is a change in attitude, but it is *mandatory* that there be a change in behavior!

Any training program should cover:

- What sexual harassment is
- What the legal restrictions against sexual harassment are
- What company policy is against sexual harassment
- How to deal with sexual harassment
- How to make a complaint
- How complaints are dealt with
- What corrective action will be taken

Supervisory employees should be trained to be responsible for:

- Reporting any evidences of sexual harassment

- Assisting in investigating and resolving formal and informal complaints

- Taking immediate and appropriate action to correct or discipline

Each employee should be trained to:

- Insure that his or her conduct does not sexually harass any employee, applicant, or outsider visiting the work place

- Insure that his or her conduct does not sexually harass any person encountered outside of the work place during working hours

- Cooperate in investigating complaints

- Cooperate to prevent and eliminate sexual harassment

- Maintain a working environment free from sexual harassment

An employee manual or handbook will act as the basic text for it should contain the company's sexual harassment policy, procedures for making a complaint, procedures for hearing a complaint, and what action will be taken if the complaint is valid. In-house seminars may be held to review the contents of the sexual harassment section of the manual and to allow for questions and discussion.

In-house workshops may be held where participants may be more involved through role play involving sexual overtures and hostile environment. Did they react appropriately? Was there sexual harassment involved? Was there evil intent or unacceptable behavior? Group discussion can follow each scenario. Role playing can include filing a complaint and the hearing that follows. Discussion about the proper action to be taken can make for lively debate.

If no one feels qualified or at ease within the company, outside consultants may be hired.

New education materials and video tapes are being developed and marketed. They may be bought or rented for use in training programs.

Step 8: Publicizing the policy

Once a company has formulated its policy, the program and the procedures that accompany it should be given maximum publicity. They should be introduced at a staff meeting that everyone attends, published in the employee manual or handbook, and displayed on the company bulletin boards. All new employees should get the information. A training program should be ongoing so that no employee, new or old, is uninformed. Information should be reviewed annually with all staff.

Step 9: Evaluation

A yearly evaluation should be made of policy and procedures. Input should come from all staff. Is it adequate? What changes should be made? Have there been grievances because of any action taken?

Changes should be made based on the evaluation and then introduced to staff. All printed material should be changed to reflect the new procedures. Changes should be monitored so they can be evaluated the following year.

All new laws and governmental guidelines concerning sexual harassment should be kept up to date and the necessary changes made to comply.

OTHER TITLES IN THE
SELF-COUNSEL BUSINESS SERIES
BY JACQUELINE DUNCKEL

THE BUSINESS GUIDE TO EFFECTIVE SPEAKING
Making presentations, using audio-visuals, and dealing with the media
by Jacqueline Dunckel and Elizabeth Parnham

Give dynamic speeches, presentations, and media interviews. When you are called upon to speak in front of your business colleagues, or asked to represent your company in front of the media, do you communicate your thoughts effectively? Or do you become tongue-tied, nervous, and worry about misrepresenting yourself and your business?

Effective communication has always been the key to business success, and this book provides a straightforward approach to developing techniques to improve your on-the-job speaking skills. This book is as easy to pick up and use as a quick reference for a specific problem as it is to read from cover to cover. Whether you want to know how to deal with the media, when to use visual aids in a presentation, or how to prepare for chairing a meeting, this book will answer your questions and help you regain your confidence. $7.95

Contents include:

- Preparing your presentation

- Let's look at visual aids

- Let's hear what you have to say: rehearsing

- How do you sound?

KEEPING CUSTOMERS HAPPY
Strategies for success
by Jacqueline Dunckel and Brian Taylor

You need good service to attract customers and keep them coming back, and this book provides plans and programs that have been proven successful by other businesses. No matter what kind of business you are in, this book will help increase profits through improved customer relations. $8.95

Contents include:

- Customer service — what it is and what it is not
- The "why" of customer relations
- The value of service
- Developing a profitable customer relations program
- Setting goals for your business
- Putting your plan together
- Communicating your customer relations program to your employees

GOOD ETHICS — GOOD BUSINESS
Your plan for success
by Jacqueline Dunckel

This book will take you step by step through questions and suggestions that encourage you to probe and define your ethics, case studies that allow you to test your reactions to ethical issues, and a plan for implementing your own business code of ethics. $8.95

ORDERING INFORMATION

All prices are subject to change without notice. Books are available in book, department, and stationery stores. If you cannot buy the book through a store, please use this order form. (Please print)

IN CANADA

Please send your order to the nearest location:

Self-Counsel Press, 1481 Charlotte Road,
North Vancouver, B. C. V7J 1H1

Self-Counsel Press, 8-2283 Argentia Road,
Mississauga, Ontario L5N 5Z2

Add 7% GST to the cost of the books.
Add $2.68 ($2.50 for postage & handling, $.18 GST)

IN THE U.S.A.

Please send your order to:

Self-Counsel Press Inc., 1704 N. State Street,
Bellingham, WA 98225

Add $2.50 for postage and handling.
WA residents please add 7.8% sales tax.

Name_____

Address_____

_____

Charge to:
❏Visa   ❏ MasterCard

Account Number_____

Validation Date _____

Expiry Date_____

Signature_____

❏ Check here for copy of our free catalogue.

Yes, please send me:
_____copies of **Business Guide to Effective
            Speaking,** $7.95
_____copies of **Keeping Customers Happy**, $8.95
_____copies of **Good Ethics — Good Business**, $8.95
_____copies of **Business Etiquette**, $9.95